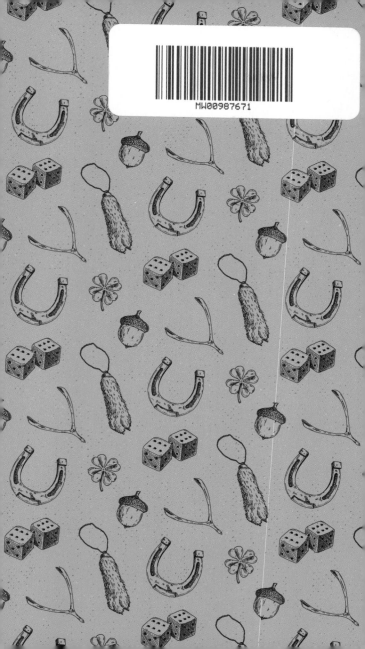

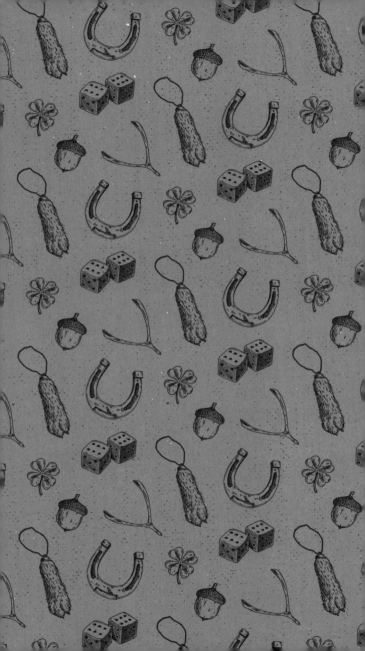

The Book of Superstitions

The Book of Superstitions

13-Digit ISBN: 978-1-64643-370-4
10-Digit ISBN: 1-64643-370-X

This book may be ordered by mail from the publisher. Please include $5.99 for postage and handling. Please support your local bookseller first!

Books published by Cider Mill Press Book Publishers are available at special discounts for bulk purchases in the United States by corporations, institutions, and other organizations.
For more information, please contact the publisher.

Cider Mill Press Book Publishers
"Where good books are ready for press"
501 Nelson Place
Nashville, TN 37214

Visit us online!
cidermillpress.com

Typography: Adobe Text, Aunt Mildred

All vectors used under official license from Shutterstock.com.

Printed in China

1 2 3 4 5 6 7 8 9 0

First Edition

The Book of Superstitions

Black Cats, Yellow Flowers,
Broken Mirrors, Cracked Sidewalks,
and More Cultural Behaviors
& Myths Explained

By Shelby El Otmani

CIDER MILL
PRESS

BOOK
PUBLISHERS

Contents

Introduction

Whenever my life feels particularly chaotic, I force myself to adopt a morning routine. By 6 o'clock, give or take, I should be awake. I give myself half an hour to squeeze in some yoga, and then I make a cup of coffee—freshly ground, French press. By 7 o'clock, I sit down at my computer, look through the local newspaper for about 15 minutes, and then I begin working.

It's not much, but these rituals give me a sense of control that lasts the rest of the day, as well as a sense of accomplishment for setting myself up for success. Sure, I know there's nothing about these rituals that guarantees good fortune, never mind a "good day" (whatever that even is). But they certainly make me feel like I'm in a good place and, most of the time, that's more than half the battle.

I can tell you this: I've never had a particularly horrible day after following my morning routine, so maybe it is lucky after all.

I'm willing to bet that you, too, have your own rituals and routines that you use to ground yourself. Maybe every Friday you meet up with friends at a particular bar so you can catch up and gripe about the workweek. Maybe every morning you stop at the same coffee shop and order the same drink to kick off your day. I'm also willing to bet there's a sense of comfort, control, and reliability attached to these actions, a feeling that makes even the most mundane habits worth maintaining.

After all, what if you don't do them and something terrible happens?

I'd argue that you can think about superstitions in the very same way.

Maybe you believe you need to knock on wood after you brag to avoid any negative repercussions for having the audacity to boast.

Maybe you believe that you must always shave your left leg before your right, otherwise you will destroy the relatively stable and predictable course your life has taken thus far.

Or perhaps you completely avoid cooking on the stove-top because you genuinely believe that if you turn it on, you'll accidently blow up your entire house.

Just to set the record straight, these are all totally hypothetical and definitely do not reflect the author's own irrational beliefs and/or delusions ...

A superstition is a belief, action, or practice that has no basis in fact but is nonetheless treated as legitimate conduct by an individual or society at large. Whether you consider yourself a skeptical, science-driven logician or a spiritual soul who's always tapped into the vibe, I'm willing to bet that you hold at least a couple beliefs that are not based upon anything more than hearsay, anxiety, or bad juju. These beliefs allow us to navigate the ceaseless chaos of our lives while also supplying the invaluable feeling that misfortune can be avoided and luck bolstered if we just follow a few simple steps, or avoid certain behaviors altogether.

That's hardly how life works, of course. And yet, just about every person on the planet, regardless of their nationality, race, gender, or religion, has at least one superstition that they follow closely to ward off misfortune, from crossing their fingers to saying "bless you" after someone sneezes.

As futile as they may seem, I think it's a mistake to completely dismiss these beliefs and how they help us make sense of our lives. The magical thinking and storytelling that have perpetuated superstitions over centuries and across borders are fundamental parts of the way humans interpret the world. When we fail to acknowledge the role they continue to play in our lives, we can become complacent, vulnerable. Just look at how powerful misinformation has become even in our ultra-educated, increasingly secular, cosmopolitan age. While many contemporary developments have transformed the way we inform and interact with each other for the better, I believe they have also provided us a false sense of security, allowing us to believe that every question can be answered, every fear dismissed, and every hurdle overcome with just a few keystrokes.

Now, none of this is to say that superstitions are perfect, unproblematic solutions. But just as a series of small, controlled burns prove effective at preventing larger, catastrophic forest fires from occurring, perhaps these small beliefs and practices keep our thoughts from carrying us over the edge. Instead of a deficiency in our programming, superstitions can be seen as ways to remain grounded in the wisdom of the past while also tapping into the incredible potential that a simple story provides, a power that can spirit us through chaos and uncertainty.

It is my hope that, by tracing the origins of some of our most common superstitions and the psychology that informs them, we can begin to find comfort in the fact that fear, loneliness, and doubt are not insurmountable. They have plagued us for the entirety of our existence, and will no doubt continue as forces to be reckoned with. As this book shows time and again, our rituals—supernatural or otherwise—are up to this task, providing a framework we can exist within, and carrying us past our unease so that we can focus upon those things that lend weight, meaning, and joy to our lives.

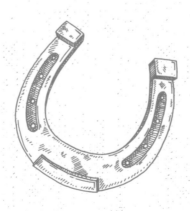

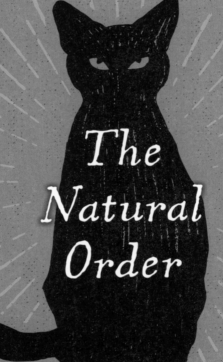

The
Natural
Order

Black Cats

I can't think of a better way to kick things off than with a discussion of black cats and all of the superstitions swirling around them. Whether you're a cat person or a dog person, super religious or a stone-cold atheist, you've probably heard that seeing a black cat is a bad omen. Should such a misfortune befall you, immediately spit over your left shoulder to reverse the curse.

Even though it's a well-known myth, the dark legend behind black cats is far from ubiquitous. In fact, some people consider black cats a sign of good luck and relish the fortune of having one cross their path.

How can that be? Well, before we dive into these conflicting beliefs, let's look at how the "black cats being a bad omen" myth got started. Black cats have been associated with all things haunted, spooky, and evil in the West for centuries for a couple reasons, starting with the basic tenets of Paganism. One of the foundational beliefs of the religion was a deep respect for the natural world. As it so happened, many Pagans (who happened to be women) also tended to keep animals as pets. Cats were particularly common because of their independent natures and connection to wildlife. This connection between Pagans and animals was emphasized in a particularly aggressive campaign from the Catholic Church that sought to drive Paganism out of Europe by linking it to Satanism and dark magic. That campaign led to centuries of religious persecution against alleged witches (i.e., regular women who did not abide by the rules and standards of the Catholic Church).

Around the thirteenth century, black cats became a target of this push and were said to be an incarnation of Satan himself. As far-fetched and unconvincing as that may sound, cats have had an enduring reputation as divine and supernatural beings throughout human history. Ancient Egyptians worshipped cats as gods, and even honored them with mummification after their deaths. Several European civilizations also held cats in high regard. Even today, cats have a reputation for being independent, haughty, and regal, which creates the sense that they are in touch with a power we mere mortals cannot possibly fathom. So, a claimed satanic link would have been taken seriously—especially since it came straight from Pope Gregory IX.

At the same time, there's a long-standing belief in the color black being associated with darkness and evil (see page 68). The combination of all these beliefs along with the manufactured fear and mystery surrounding non-Christian belief would have likely fueled a moral panic. In that, and any, panic, it's easy for mundane facts, such as ownership of a black cat, to take on a sinister meaning.

The link between black cats and witchcraft eventually became so strong and widespread that people began to believe that these cats were witches themselves. From here, you can see why a black cat crossing your path is considered bad luck—essentially, it means you are being followed by a witch, and are likely already under their spell.

These days, witchcraft and magic have become far more accepted in Europe and North America, and the associated spooky imagery is so common that it has been rendered harmless. Black cats, once the spawn of Satan, have regained their wide appeal, though some wariness lingers.

But as mentioned in the beginning, not everyone associates black cats with spookiness. In Japan, black cats are seen as good luck for single women specifically, increasing the odds of attracting a great romantic partner. Whether it's because cats possess magical powers or because they're just adorable is unclear. Though it's probably a bit of both.

Full Moon Fever

Weird things just seem to happen more frequently when the Moon is full. I remember being in school and hearing my teachers remark that it must be a full Moon because their students were acting particularly unruly that day. Apparently, puberty and a full Moon don't mix. Sure enough, it often seemed that these remarks lined up with an incoming full Moon either that very night or just a day or two away. And, while the physical effects of the Moon on Earth are clear— its gravitational pull controls the planet's tides—it seems to have some influence on our psyches, as well.

The belief that a full Moon brings chaos is ingrained in just about every culture across the globe, so much so that the concept has made its way into our language. In English, the word "lunatic" traditionally refers to someone "affected with a seriously disordered state of mind," and begets other derogatory terms associated with mental illness, including "looney" and "looney bin." The less problematic and colloquial definition we've adapted today is more along the lines of "wildly foolish." Either way, the main root of the word—"luna"—is a direct reference to the Latin word for "moon." So "lunatic" literally means "moon sick."

Etymology lesson aside, first accounts of this so-called moon sickness can be found among the Ancient Greeks, who drew rudimentary connections between the Moon and the tides. The idea that the Moon held sway over earthly goings-on was extended to the human mind by Hippocrates, as the famed physician noted the alleged effects of the Moon on peoples' odd behaviors and mental health issues. That ancient diagnosis was an influential one since centuries later, the impact of a full Moon upon one's decision-making was seen as a valid defense in English courts.

All that leads us to today, where if you exasperatedly exclaim "must be a full Moon" to a full room of friends or colleagues, most will know exactly what you mean—particularly if you work in healthcare. There have been several surveys and studies done at hospitals to see what superstitions persist among the staff, and in many cases, most participants believed that their patients were far more chaotic and aggressive when there was a full Moon.

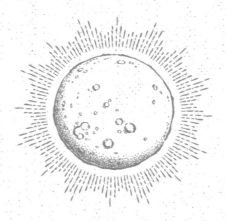

Of course, it's no surprise that this superstition runs particularly hot in the healthcare industry and the education system—as both fields are notorious for staff burnout and overall dissatisfaction.

I also think there's a self-fulfilling piece of this belief. Sort of like how people swear that saying "good luck" or "Macbeth" at the theater (see pages 150 and 151, respectively) is terrible luck because they've seen the resulting misfortunes with their own eyes. It's more likely that people are looking for strange behaviors during a full Moon because of the lore behind this superstition.

It's also possible that people use the full Moon as an excuse to let their inhibitions down more than usual. That's not necessarily a problem—just try not to do anything that will land you in a hospital, if you can help it.

Rabbit, Rabbit

If you're coming off a bad month and need some better luck in the next, don't forget to say "Rabbit, rabbit."

The habit of saying "rabbit, rabbit" (or "white rabbit") is most common in the British Isles and North America. People believe that saying this plucky phrase at the beginning of the month will grant you 30 days of good luck and prosperity. But there are some rules to make it work. For one, it must be said on the first day of the month and it absolutely must be the very first thing you say aloud.

The rules are clear, but there doesn't seem to be a consensus on how or why people started saying it. Some of the first accounts of the phrase being associated with good luck were recorded at the beginning of the twentieth century. The very first mention is from a British periodical called *The Academy* in which one person (going by the mysterious moniker D. M.) submits the following question: "Many children believe that if, on the first day of the month, they succeed in saying 'Rabbits' before it is said to them, they will receive a present. What is the origin of this myth?" A few years later, in 1909, another British periodical known as *Notes and*

Queries published a submission from someone who describes their daughter yelling "rabbits" at the start of every month in hopes of bringing herself good luck, and asks if this is a historical custom.

While neither inquiry seems to have generated a definitive answer, it makes sense that a rabbit would be the animal chosen to manifest good luck for an entire month. As we see with the history of the lucky rabbit's foot (see page 55), these nimble little creatures have been considered symbols of good fortune, longevity, and new beginnings in many parts of the world for centuries, in part because of their incredible speed, fertility, and burrowing habits, the latter of which made people think they were connected to the spirits in the afterlife.

Beyond superstition, rabbits have been used as symbols of awakening and rebirth in *Alice's Adventures in Wonderland*, *The Matrix*, and other narratives where the protagonist is searching for something new, different, and/or utterly mind-blowing. Who wouldn't want every month to be full of surprises and new insights that change the way you think of life for the better? Sounds like good luck to me! It's also much safer than taking a pill from someone you just met.

Crows & Ravens

You don't have to be a horror fan to know that these black birds have a reputation for foreshadowing gruesome ends. From Edgar Allen Poe's "The Raven" to more modern hits like *The Sopranos* and

28 Days Later, crows and ravens have become messengers of bad things to come across many cultures. This symbolism paired with the fact that both crows and ravens are scavengers (i.e., they feast on dead animals) has made way for more than a couple superstitions to gather around these birds—namely, that seeing a crow is a sign that death is near.

The suspicion around crows and ravens is surprisingly common across the globe and among different cultures. Seen as everything from pure evil to playful tricksters, these birds have quite a reputation, one that extends from mythology and folklore all the way to us. For the Ancient Greeks, ravens were closely associated with Apollo and were allegedly all white until the god used the birds to spy on his lover, who had been cheating on him. In his anger, Apollo turned the birds black, a color steeped in stigma itself (see page 68). As a result, crows became most closely associated with Apollo's wrath. Combine that with Apollo recognizing that the birds would make great spies, and crows don't exactly seem like an animal you'd want hanging around.

In recent years, however, both crows and ravens have received more positive attention than ever, having been recognized as extremely intelligent. Several studies have shown that the birds are capable of high-level problem solving and can use tools (such as sticks) to retrieve treats from difficult-to-reach places. Studies also suggest that ravens are capable of planning ahead for multiple future outcomes beyond just instinctual survival, a trait formerly believed to exist only among some primates (including humans). If that doesn't impress (or terrify) you, ravens have also exhibited the ability to hold grudges and favor some humans over others.

If you don't believe me, just head over to TikTok's #crowtok and see for yourself how some folks have befriended these intelligent feathered friends.

But these abilities are not news to some—Native Americans have admired crows and ravens for centuries. Where most see morbidity and spookiness, Native Americans have traditionally admired these corvids' intelligence and ability to transform the environment around them. In addition to a host of legends about the birds, many tribes across North America have adopted either a crow or raven as a clan animal.

Based on their intelligence and incredible ability to plan, maybe there is something to the idea that crows and ravens have a few tricks to share with us.

When a Bird Hits the Window

If you're a horror fan, you're probably familiar with Ari Aster's *Hereditary*. The film tackles the horrors of inheritance through a psychological and supernatural lens. One scene toward the beginning of the film shows Charlie Graham, a shy young girl prone to a tongue-clicking tic, sitting in her classroom as she and her classmates take a test. The silence is broken by a bird hitting the window, an incident that leaves a gruesome bloodstain on the glass and freaks out all of the students, except for Charlie. After class, Charlie heads over to the bush where the bird fell and uses a pair of scissors to cut its head off. She then slips the severed head in her pocket. It's gross, unsettling and, of course, a harbinger of the horrific things to come. But not at all in the way you expect.

I bring up this scene not just because I'll take any excuse to talk about the film, but because I think it's a perfect example of how a superstition can mean more than one thing at a time. The most common belief behind a bird hitting a window, at least in the West, is that it's a sign of approaching misfortune—particularly illness and death.

But I think "death" here is open to interpretation, especially when we think about it in the context of a movie like *Hereditary*. Sure, it's easy and even understandable to interpret it as a sign of a loss approaching—we see this depicted in the movie, quite clearly and traumatically. But death can take many forms. It might be the end of a relationship, the loss of a job, the loss of mobility due to illness or injury. But as we see in the film, and in life, the end is also the beginning—for better or worse.

This open interpretation of a bird hitting a window is particularly common among spiritual and psychic communities. Often the shock of a bird hitting the window is read as a sign that a loved one—usually deceased—is trying to send you an important message regarding your life. As such, it's important to take stock of your life in that moment and decide what you're lacking or what you have too much of. Have you been putting off that doctor's appointment? How are you feeling about your closest relationships?

Whether you believe this superstition or not, I think the shock of a bird hitting the window provides just the right jolt to snap you into the present. In these rare moments of concern, surprise, and perhaps even sadness for the poor bird, we can take a moment to appreciate how fragile everything is and how, without ever seeing it coming, the world can toss up a huge barrier that changes the trajectory of our entire lives.

Black Sheep, (Don't) Come Home

All sheep are cute, but I think black sheep are especially cute. I mean, they know that an all-black ensemble is a killer look, and they're not afraid to stand out. That's my kind of ruminant.

In Scotland, however, where they are a seriously bad omen, I'll keep this affinity to myself.

Because the color black is so closely linked to Satan in Scottish culture, farmers believe that the birth of a black sheep is a sign that the rest of the flock is doomed to die.

Furthermore, if a sheep gives birth to twins with black faces, farmers know to expect a bad lambing season. It is interesting that I could not find any evidence that the farmers did anything to get rid of the black sheep or reverse the alleged curse they put on the rest of the flock. It's as if they simply accepted the decree and cut their losses.

As you've probably guessed, this superstition gave birth to the term "black sheep in the family," though the phrase has developed to where one member is not viewed as a curse on the entire clan, but an odd duck. It's even a term that people might wear proudly. But a more precise definition is that the people around the supposed "black sheep" consider them discomforting or disreputable. And, if you happen to be the black sheep in your family, you probably know it's not all it's cracked up to be. Life is tough enough, you know? To feel alienated from those you're supposed to be closest to makes it that much more difficult.

Interestingly, the Scots are accepting of the black

sheep if the whole breed is black—the Hebridean line consists of small, black sheep and is quite popular in the country. It's just the odd ones out that spook them.

Sacred Seabirds

Imagine packing a lunch for a day at the beach and having it swiped out of your hands by a seagull. Such a violation may make you feel "avianicidal" (a word that doesn't exist but, as this all-too-believable situation shows, absolutely should). But it'd be wise to resist the urge to seek revenge on your hungry, feathered foe. Aside from being morally objectionable, killing a seabird is considered extremely bad luck.

This belief is one of many superstitions resulting from life at sea. Centuries ago, sailors from Europe and North America came to believe that seabirds, particularly albatrosses, possessed supernatural abilities because of how they could maneuver through the sky without flapping their wings. Today, we know that the birds use air currents from the water to propel themselves. But back then, seeing birds gliding through the air probably looked a lot like magic. So that, combined with the albatross' attraction to the sea, led sailors to believe that these birds carried the souls of deceased sailors. Thus, killing an albatross ultimately meant you were harming a fellow sailor, the consequences of which ranged from personal inconveniences to the watery demise of your entire crew.

A likely origin for this superstition comes from a 1726 autobiography by George Shelvocke called *Voyage Around the World by Way of the Great South Sea*. Shelvocke, a former sailor, describes a black albatross that had been following the ship for weeks, effortlessly gliding around the ship as if it knew the vessel intimately. He then explains how one of his shipmates, in a particularly foul mood due to the bad weather and a bit of homesickness, fatally shot the bird over fears that it was responsible for the grey cloud hanging over the boat.

This moment in literature made way for other writers and poets to adapt the symbolism of an albatross and potentially disastrous outcomes, leading to the superstition that many sailors, fishermen, and other sea-faring folk still believe today. The superstition even applies to other, more common seabirds, including seagulls. So powerful is this myth that it has also made its way on shore—the expression "to have an albatross around your neck" is a direct reference to this enduring superstition. Used to characterize an unwanted burden, the idiom was coined by Samuel Taylor Coleridge in the 1798 poem "The Rime of the Ancient Mariner," which was inspired by Shelvocke's account. The poem describes a sailor who recalls killing a seabird and the misfortunes it brought him and the rest of his crew:

Ah! well a-day!

What evil looks

Had I from old and young!

Instead of the cross, the Albatross

About my neck was hung.

Let this be a gentle warning: next time you head to the beach and are besieged by birds, let your lunch go. It's a small price to pay, considering the potential consequences.

Groundhog Day

Every February 2nd is the same: wake up, roll out of bed, turn on the news. And there he is: Punxsutawney Phil—that famous little groundhog with an astonishing aptitude for meteorology (so we're told). And despite the repetition and predictability of the event itself, the question still grips us: Will Phil see his shadow this year? Or will winter end on schedule? We sit rapt, all eyes on a tiny Pennsylvania town, waiting for Phil to pop his head out of his hole and reveal what the coming weeks have in store for us. And we wait. And we wait. And we wait.

Groundhog Day has been celebrated in the United States since 1887, when the original Punxsutawney Phil became our national weather rat. The tradition itself, however, stems from a mix of long-standing Christian tradition and good old-fashioned American marketing.

Before Groundhog Day, there was Candlemas. This German holiday was celebrated every year around the midpoint between the winter solstice and the spring equinox (incidentally, sometime in February). During Candlemas, the church would hand out a bunch of blessed candles to people who'd gathered in the town. If the weather was nice as the people held their candles, they were in for a few more weeks of rough winter conditions. But if the weather was cloudy and gray, they could rejoice that spring was on the way. In other iterations of observing the holiday, people would turn to the wisdom of either a badger or a hedgehog to confirm what the rest of the season held. Sound familiar?

As Germans began immigrating to the United States, and to Pennsylvania in particular, they brought this weather-predicting tradition with them. But as badgers were hard to come by in rural Pennsylvania, they had to find another rodent to rely on. Enter the groundhog.

Eventually, local newspapers in Punxsutawney began to pick up on this quirky tradition, and in 1886 began advertising their own event scheduled for February 2, 1887, a gathering to be staged with the help of the members of the Punxsutawney Groundhog Club. The club publicly announced that one groundhog in particular, dubbed Punxsutawney

Phil, was the only true magical, weather-predicting groundhog, leading to lore that the Punxsutawney Phil we see today is the very same Phil from the original Groundhog Day.

Today, thousands of people gather on Gobbler's Notch, just outside of Punxsutawney, to see Phil's prediction. Even more people watch on TV or online. And these days, other towns across the United States have gotten in on the act, selecting their own groundhog to predict the weather. Though I'm not sure if I trust these Phil impersonators. If we're going to take our weather pattern predictions from a rodent, I'd prefer it comes from an OG. Punxsutawney Phil or bust!

The Owls Are Not What They Seem

David Lynch was onto something when he turned owls into a spooky motif in *Twin Peaks*, using these adorable raptors to suggest the presence of an all-seeing evil spirit in the titular town.

In the no-less Lynchian real world, owls may be seen as good luck, bad luck, or even a sign of approaching death depending on where you live. Regardless, all of the mythology surrounding these impressive birds are influenced by owls' rumored connection to the supernatural. For instance, in some cultures, owls are considered sacred animals, symbolizing wisdom and intelligence. The Ancient Greeks often depicted Athena, Greek goddess of wisdom, with an owl companion. But in Christian Europe, owls came to be associated with witchcraft, due to a belief that witches could transform into the birds. The Christian hysteria over witches is not the only set of beliefs that cast owls in a negative light, as several Native American tribes consider owls a symbol of the god of death.

Clearly, the owl is viewed as a powerful force throughout the world, and this appraisal has given rise to many superstitions, such as the belief that hearing an owl hoot three times will bring you bad luck. Or that an owl landing on the roof of a house is a sign that someone in that house will soon die.

While we're on the subject of death, fans of true crime will be familiar with "the owl theory" in the famous case of Kathleen and Michael Peterson, where Kathleen Peterson was mysteriously found dead at the bottom of her staircase, covered in blood, and with a number of gashes on her scalp. Michael Peterson was found guilty following a controversial trial, eventually granted an appeal, and ultimately pleaded guilty to avoid further jail time. What's interesting is that none of the theories offered to support or eliminate Michael's involvement in his wife's death made much sense. Eventually, the couple's neighbor suggested that an owl may have attacked Kathleen, and that when she tried to clean up in her upstairs bedroom, she fell down the stairs and bled out. As wild as it sounds, there's a good amount of evidence supporting this theory. And, given the (death-related) legends about owls, maybe it's not nearly as wild as it seems.

Snow Day Wishes

I was a very dedicated student growing up. Like Hermione Granger, I feared a bad grade or evaluation more than I feared death itself. I had an insatiable desire to learn, and school was the place to do that. But even I wasn't immune to the overwhelming joy of a snow day.

Years since my last lesson, I can still feel the rush of excitement and relief that would course through my body upon seeing the name of my school scroll across the bottom of the TV screen with the word "Closed" beside it. And I know I'm not alone. When kids shifted to remote learning during the COVID-19 pandemic, there were several think pieces wondering if snow days would be a thing of the past, and what

this loss entailed for the fragile youth of America. Considering all of the hardships caused by the pandemic, these essays seemed a little much—but they were right to point out that the loss was not insignificant.

Now that we're getting back to normal, snow days have (mostly) returned. And according to families across North America, there are several ways to arrange for that magical moment when we learn that classes have been canceled. Known as a "Snow Day Wish" in some corners, this superstition consists of the various rituals a child can perform that are bound to get school canceled due to inclement weather, from wearing your pajamas inside-out to flushing ice cubes down the toilet.

It's not clear exactly where these rituals started, but they are obviously closely connected to humanity's long history of individuals trying to summon favorable weather conditions. You're probably already familiar with the concept of a rain dance, which has been practiced by indigenous people across North America. But ritualistic behavior meant to attract specific weather has also been practiced in Europe and Asia for centuries. And, following the line of thinking that people develop superstitions in order to control the uncontrollable, these rites make a lot of sense. After all, it's hard to think of anything more unpredictable than the weather!

As far as the Snow Day Wishes go, there are a variety of rituals you can perform. If wearing your PJs inside out sounds unappealing, you could put a spoon under your pillow or eat a bowl of ice cream before you head to bed. That last one sounds good enough that I'm going to try it out this evening, even though snow days aren't something I can really hope for these days.

Morning Dew in May

For centuries, people in Scotland believed there was no better skin care routine than waking up at the crack of dawn on the first of May to wash their faces with morning dew.

The thinking behind this May Day tradition can be linked back to Druidry, which was once the dominant spiritual practice among the Celts. Druids believed in cultivating close relationships with nature and the environment, and would therefore perform different rituals to raise the odds of better harvesting seasons. But one of their main beliefs was that moisture produced in the natural world was innately holy and a necessary element of vitality and growth.

The ritual at the center of the May Dew belief was a festival known as Beltane, which usually took place on May 1, to celebrate the transition from spring to summer. The celebration involved massive bonfires and feasts, and all houses in the community would douse the fires that had kept them warm over the winter and light a new one using flames from the communal bonfire, clearing out the old to make way for the new.

On Beltane morning, people would wake early in the morning, head to the nearest field or hill, and cleanse themselves with the dew produced after Beltane. Doing so was said to ensure beauty, good health, and good luck for the new year.

The tradition remained popular for hundreds of years and continued to draw thousands of people out of their homes and into the wet grass each May 1 well into the 1960s. But today, hardly anyone in Scotland participates—at least in the cities. And, considering all of the pollutants we've saddled the environment with over the last few centuries, maybe that's for the best.

Breathtaking Cats

Since the seventeenth century, many new parents have been wary of having cats in the same house as their babies, fearing that the cat will literally steal the child's breath. And no, I don't just mean black cats.

All cats are suspect, regardless of color.

This belief relies heavily upon the negative reputation cats have developed over the centuries. Between black cats being linked to witchcraft (see page 11) and cats' generally aloof and capricious manner, many people don't fully trust felines. Add in how grieving parents, desperate to make sense of their crumbling world after their child's death, can understandably exercise some wild logic, and it's not entirely surprising that this myth would hold strong through the generations.

One theory regarding the origins of this particular piece of anti-cat propaganda suggests that cats are attracted to the smell of milk from the baby's feedings and will climb into the crib and smother the child, while others say that the cats are lashing out because they are furious about no longer being the center of attention. And, like most superstitions, there have been several anecdotes over the years that seem to "prove" the validity of the belief, including a coroner's report published in the eighteenth century that cited a breath-stealing cat as the cause of one baby's death.

Thankfully, modern medicine has helped us understand that issues like Sudden Infant Death Syndrome (SIDS) can cause a healthy baby to die seemingly out of nowhere, and this breathtaking conviction isn't quite as potent as it once was. But that still doesn't prevent some moms from being wary about having cats around their offspring.

Lucky Fliegenpilz

Finish this sentence: Mushrooms are _____.

Depending on where you're from as well as what your preferences and experiences are, maybe you finished the sentence with "delicious on pizza," or "downright disgusting." Some of you may have even said "the best trip of your life." Hey man, no judgment. That's cool.

If you're German or of German descent though, perhaps you finished the sentence with "lucky".

The fliegenpilz, also known as fly agaric, is that cartoonish red mushroom with white spots that occasionally sprouts in forests across the Northern Hemisphere. It's basically the mushroom you'll see popping up in things like The Smurfs and the Mario Bros. franchise. In

Germany and other parts of Europe, finding one of these mushrooms in the wild is the equivalent of finding a penny heads up on the ground (see page 61). Should you stumble upon one, you might even be called a glückspilz ("lucky mushroom")!

These red-and-white mushrooms are considered lucky in part because of the trying circumstances in which they grow. Because of the way their roots develop, they can only grow at the base of fir trees, which are most often associated with Christmas. As such, replicas of these bright red toadstools are often incorporated into Christmas decorations in Central Europe, including as ornaments and decorations for the scrumptious yule logs (just make sure they're not the real thing, because they're actually quite poisonous). However, while the fliegenpilz is most prominently displayed during the Christmas season, it serves as a good luck charm year-round.

As I mentioned, the term glückspilz is closely tied to the fliegenpilz, but it wasn't always that way. It was originally a somewhat derogatory term for someone who had become wealthy and climbed the social ladder overnight—much like calling someone "new money" in English. Allegedly, sometime in the nineteenth century, the term took on a more positive connotation. From where I stand, as someone who's never had the opportunity to be branded a glückspilz, the term is tinged with envy either way. I know I feel a little green when people find lucky objects in the wild!

Red, White, and Doom

Growing up, I always had flowers in the house. My father's job revolved around exotic flowers, and at least once a week he would have a bundle of colorful stems from Costa Rica or Singapore in a vase on the kitchen table. The joy of seeing a new arrangement never got old, and to this day a vase of flowers on the table provides a sense of comfort and contentedness. I'm sure I'm not alone.

The warm and fuzzy feeling created by a bouquet is probably why getting flowers when you're under the weather is so heartening—it's nice to bring a little beauty back into your life in those moments where everything seems to be teetering. But, if you're thinking of lifting someone's spirits during a hospital stay, there's something you should know: never combine red and white flowers in a bouquet. Otherwise, you may actually be sending someone to an early grave.

This superstition, which hails from England, is based on the fact that red and white, particularly in the context of a hospital, are very reminiscent of blood and bandages. People take the myth so seriously, in fact, that some florists in the country will refuse to make a red-and-white arrangement if they know it's going to someone in the hospital.

It's interesting to note, too, that it's not necessarily the recipient of the red-and-white arrangement that is in danger of dying—the bad luck can spread to any patient in the ward. So, unless you can live with yourself after taking out an entire wing of people, stick to just one color. And while you're at it, make sure it's an odd number of stems (see page 46).

Lucky Bird Poop

Sure, it stinks. But bird poop falling on your head may be the very best thing that ever happened to you.

If you've ever experienced this particularly awful bombardment on your way to work or a date, you've probably been reassured that you shouldn't complain because it's good luck. However, if you've ever personally been violated by bird feces (like I was one time in Milan), it feels like anything but fortunate. Of all the places that poop could have landed, why did it end up on your dome?

It turns out, that question is the lifeblood of this superstition.

Indeed, a bird has all the world to use as a toilet. But let's break this down. The chances of a bird flying or perching directly above you are long in themselves. Now combine those long odds with the likelihood that the bird, at that very moment, decides to relieve

itself. Account for wind and other factors, and the probability of getting blessed by bird feces becomes astronomical.

But why is it necessarily good luck? Is it because of its longshot nature, combined with the fact that it is coming from on high? Why not associate it with bad luck or misfortune, as it certainly feels that way?

Aside from my cynical theory that this superstition is just a way for people to keep you from crying in public, there is a strong association between feces and good fortune.

In addition to other scat-related superstitions (like how it's apparently good luck to step in dog poop), whale feces, known as ambergris, has long been a valued resource because of its sought-after scent (it supposedly smells like vanilla after it's been floating around in the ocean for decades). As of August 2022, a gram of whale poop costs more than a gram of gold! And while a whale couldn't be more different than a bird, the point stands that there is value in excrement—even for humans. After all, much information about our health and well-being is contained in our waste. And I'd say that's pretty precious.

Perhaps the superstition is a way of reminding you that you are part of the natural order, or a sign something good will have to happen in order to balance things out. Or maybe it's just a long-winded way of trying to make you feel better about getting shat on by a bird.

Numerology, Charms & Fortune

Unlucky 13

I sort of feel bad for the number 13. It technically did nothing wrong, and yet many people around the world have an intense aversion to it.

Fear around the number 13 is so strong that people throughout the world have gone to great lengths to avoid it. There are even some buildings across North America that do not have a thirteenth floor. Well, they do, of course. But they don't label it as the thirteenth. They jump from the twelfth to the four-teenth, hoping to spare anyone the misfortune of spending a day or an evening immersed in 13-ness.

This number's inauspicious origins are a bit hazy, but some believe this number is unlucky simply because it comes after the number 12, which many people, influenced by Christian doctrine, consider to be a symbol of completeness and divine authority.

One step past it, and all hell breaks loose. Simple as that, apparently. Now, the anxiety around Friday the 13th specifically dates back to the Bible, where Fridays have an especially rueful reputation—it's sup-posedly the day when Adam and Eve ate the forbid-den fruit from the Tree of Knowledge, the day of the week when Cain murdered his brother, Abel, and also the day Jesus was crucified. During the late nineteenth century, this inauspicious day and the fearsome 13 were combined into one super-unlucky occurrence.

The superstition grew as it was passed down through

the generations, with more and more people on the lookout for unlucky things that took place on Friday the 13th or that somehow involve the number 13. Of course, there are plenty of examples of unfortunate events: there were 13 people present at the Last Supper; the Apollo 13 incident happened on April 13, 1970; and more recently, the terrorist attacks in Paris that occurred during November 2015 and left 130 innocent civilians dead took place on Friday the 13th.

While Friday the 13th gets most of the attention, it's not the only unlucky day in the world. In Spain and Greece, for example, it's actually Tuesday the 13th that's considered unlucky because of its connection to the sack of Constantinople in 1204, the culmination of the Fourth Crusade.

Whatever the day of the week, it's probably best to just keep your head down whenever the 13th day of the month arrives, and hope you get through unscathed.

Knock on Wood

At this point, knocking on wood after mentioning some instance when fortune visited you is basically a compulsion. Whether you knock on natural wood, a wood-like substance, your head, or just say the phrase out loud, this superstition has been deeply rooted in the collective psyche for centuries to ensure that you hang onto your good fortune.

Early pagans and other cultures across the globe

believed that spirits lived in trees. As such, trees became symbols of divinity, and were often used in rituals. One theory suggests that people began touching trees as a means of asking the spirits residing within for favors. Another theory is that people would knock on the wood to pick up the good vibes within.

It's worth noting that the connection between wood and spirituality can also be found in Christianity. Back in Medieval Europe, after paganism had largely been outlawed, churches across the continent linked wood with Jesus's cross, and some went so far as to claim that their church contained a fragment of the famed cross. As a result, churchgoers would knock on the wooden part of the church for good luck.

Today, the act is done not so much to gain favor or worship, as it is a mystical insurance policy. Much like pagan home-owners who would knock on the wood of their homes to send nosy spirits away before they could ruin a streak of good luck, people today knock on wood to avoid having some bit of fortune reversed. For example, if you start talking about something ill-fated that could theoretically happen and disrupt your charmed life, actually knocking on wood or even saying "knock on wood" as you proceed to rap your knuckles on a table or doorway gives many people a sense of safety from said bad thing happening to them.

So, if something good happens to you, don't be afraid to toot your own horn a little. But be sure to acknowledge that your luck could be stripped away in an instant by giving the nearest tree a knock.

Lucky Horseshoe

Any guesses as to how horseshoes got a reputation for being lucky? No, seriously. I'm really asking. It seems like there are a million potential reasons for why horseshoes are considered lucky, making it difficult to pinpoint one definitive origin. The narratives surrounding these charms are so diverse that people can't even agree on which way to hang them so you actually reap the benefits!

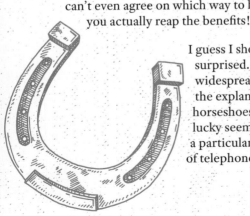

I guess I shouldn't be surprised. Like many widespread superstitions, the explanation for why horseshoes are considered lucky seems like the end of a particularly bizarre game of telephone.

Like lucky pennies (see page 61), horseshoes are likely considered lucky in part because of the powerful connection between metal and the divine that has lived on since the Ancient Greeks. Furthermore, horseshoes have historically been crafted by a blacksmith, which was considered a lucky and magical trade, in part because their god, Hephaestus, bestowed the gift of fire on humanity.

While the reverence for metal comes from the Ancient Greeks, some theories pin the origin of the lucky horseshoe to the British Isles. As for what a lucky horseshoe is meant to do ... well, it depends on who you ask. While luck is no doubt part of the charm, some people also consider these totems a means of spiritual protection. One story goes that St. Dunstan, who worked as a blacksmith, fitted the devil with a horseshoe that hurt his hoof so much he begged the saint to take it off. But St. Dunstan wouldn't remove it until the devil promised to never cross a threshold where a horseshoe was hanging. The devil agreed, and so the horseshoe became a way to protect a household from spiritual harm and the evil eye.

From there, horseshoes have become one of the most trusted and versatile charms in the history of humanity, employed at everything from weddings to New Year's Eve celebrations. If you're interested in tapping into their considerable power, however, you should know how to use one first. Most people believe that the horseshoe should have its ends facing up in order to capture luck and keep it in the household. If it's upside down, it lets luck spill out and leaves you vulnerable. But there are other people who believe the horseshoe works either way, just with different effects: having the ends up keeps the luck in, while having it upside down sends luck out to repel evil spirits.

Wherever you fall on the horseshoe placement debate, I think it's fascinating to know that this simple act of hanging a horseshoe has such an involved and storied origin. That's a lot of luck to back you up!

Don't Even Go There

There's no shortage of superstitions centered around flowers. From avoiding giving yellow flowers to your loved one (see page 107) to not sending a red-and-white bouquet to someone in the hospital (see page 36), you may be wondering what other things you should know about giving flowers to someone without unintentionally wishing ill upon them.

Well, your list is about to get longer, because another common flower superstition is that you should never give someone an arrangement composed of an even number of flowers.

This myth is quite popular in Eastern Europe and is considered bad luck because traditionally, even-numbered arrangements were only created for funerals. As such, giving someone an even number of flowers is like wishing them dead. The only

exception to this is having thirteen
flowers in an arrangement,
because of that number's
own ominous associa-
tions, at least in the West
(see page 41).

This superstition sits in stark
contrast to the practice of giving
your beloved a dozen roses, which
is a common gift between romantic
partners in North America. But rest
assured, asking for a dozen roses (or
any flower) from a florist in Eastern
Europe will probably get you some
suspicious looks, unless the arrangement is
specifically for a funeral.

So, if you're really looking for a way out of
a relationship with someone—especially if they're
Russian or of Eastern European decent—but you
just don't have the guts to say it, you could get them
a dozen yellow roses to really drive home the point
that things aren't working out. Your message would
most likely be crystal clear, though it's probably not
the most mature way to handle things.

Broken Mirrors

Mirrors are tricky things. While we're inclined to
believe that they show us what's true, in reality there
are actually many factors that can skew the image
they display: the type of glass, the lighting in the

room, and the angle at which the mirror is hung can all affect our reflection. Even our own minds can warp the version of us that resides in the glass. Despite all of this, it's so easy to become consumed by your own image—even if you're not particularly vain.

When a mirror breaks, it's not only dangerous and messy—it's also believed to be very bad luck. In fact, as the well-known superstition goes, you'll have seven years of bad luck if you're there when the looking glass shatters.

To understand this superstition, let's look back at where this fascination with mirrors and our reflections comes from. While today many people might say that being mirror-obsessed is vain, the allure of mirrors has roots back to the Ancient Greeks, who believed that seeing yourself in these reflective surfaces could reveal your soul. Of course, this idea is illustrated in the myth of Narcissus, who was cursed to fall in love with his own reflection on the surface of a river.

It was the Romans that took the idea of looking at yourself upon the water's surface and created a fixed medium through polished metal, which was eventually upgraded to glass. Furthermore, the Romans considered mirrors as a vehicle for the gods to peer into a person's soul—you were not only discovering yourself, but also revealing yourself. Because of this spiritual link, breaking a mirror was considered a direct insult to the gods and a sign of tremendous disrespect, with seven years of rotten luck headed your way as a punishment.

But why seven years? The Romans also believed that life was regenerated every seven years. Therefore, after seven years, you were an entirely new person, no longer the clumsy and/or disrespectful one that broke the mirror. A pretty brilliant little thought technology, if you ask me.

Mirrors don't necessarily have to be broken to hold magical powers. If you're looking for something a little less dreadful than seven years of bad luck, there are several mirror-related myths dedicated to the idea that by performing certain rituals at midnight in front of one, the image of your future partner will appear (see page 169). Because if there's anything more alluring than our own image in the mirror, it's a solution to the mystery of what our future lover might look like. Just pray that the mirror doesn't shatter as that image starts to materialize.

Walking Under a Ladder

I don't think I've ever walked under a ladder. For one, it's super-dangerous. In a split-second, my anxious, morbid mind pictures all the things that could go wrong. And second, why would I want to? In what circumstance is walking under a ladder the natural move?

But honestly, the biggest influence upon my aversion to walking under ladders is the belief that it will
bring me bad luck.

This superstition is so common that
you've likely heard of it before this—
maybe you even believe it yourself.
And it's no wonder why it's become
so engrained in our beliefs; it's been
around in some form since Ancient
Egypt. The Egyptians believed
that the shape of a triangle or
pyramid in any form was sacred—
even the triangle formed by a
ladder leaning against a wall.
As a result, walking under the
ladder—and therefore through
the triangle—would besmirch
the sacred space, sullying it
with your profane, unworthy
self. This spawned a similar
belief in Christianity, which
held that the shape created
by a ladder leaning against
a wall was akin to the Holy
Trinity. That made walking under a ladder
blasphemous.

If neither of those outlooks convinces you to
stay clear of leaning ladders, this one might: hanging was a popular means of execution in Medieval
Europe, and ladders were the means by which the
condemned ascended to the noose. As such, it was

believed that the triangle created by the leaning ladder contained the souls of those who had been put to death, and walking through it could subject you to their wayward spirits.

Fortunately, if you accidentally walk under a ladder because you're too busy texting or just lost in your own thoughts, there are a couple ways to reverse the negative effects. One is to simply reverse your path by walking backwards under the ladder (just as risky, if you ask me). The other, which is a superstition in its own right, is to cross your fingers (see page 86) while you're passing underneath.

Opening Umbrellas Inside

To umbrella or not to umbrella? That's the question you inevitably ask yourself as you step out the door and notice a black cloud slowly floating toward you. You don't remember the weatherman mentioning any possibility of rain, but that ominous cloud heading your way says otherwise. Better to be safe than sorry, you think.

Or maybe you're the type who sees that menacing cloud enveloping the sky and decide that you'll leave the umbrella at home. You hate being weighed down by it, you think, and it's an even bigger problem

The Book of Superstitions

when it's all wet. You'll take your chances and head out without protection. You don't even know why you have an umbrella in the first place—you never use it!

Wherever you personally fall on the umbrella question, there's one thing we can all agree on: you should never, under any circumstance, open one indoors.

Besides being incredibly useless, opening an umbrella when you're indoors has been considered bad luck in many parts of the world for centuries. One likely source of this superstition comes from Ancient Egypt, where the upper classes used umbrellas to protect themselves from the sun rather than the rain. It was considered disrespectful to the sun god Ra, however, if these umbrellas were ever used in the shade (created by some sort of indoor or at least covered area). Legend has it that Ra would then rain terror down upon the household where the umbrella-related offense occurred.

I know, this seems counterintuitive. After all, you'd think Ra would be offended if people tried to shield themselves from his life-giving glow. But my theory is that Ra might have considered using umbrellas in the shade an insult because it looked as if the umbrella user was embracing a false god. If umbrellas became synonymous with the sun, his domain, then why would you use one in a place where there's no sunshine? It's difficult to be the sun god, no doubt, but Ra, this feels like a bit of a reach.

The umbrella myth as we know it today, though,

most likely developed around the eighteenth century, which is around the time when umbrellas came to be mass produced. Unlike modern umbrellas, however, these portable shelters were basically weapons powerful enough to poke out an eye whenever they were opened. So, from a practical standpoint, opening one in an enclosed space with a bunch of people standing around—whether it's your home, office, or in a store—could be extremely dangerous.

Even as umbrellas have evolved into something far less dangerous, the superstition has stuck around. Are people really still that concerned about Ra cursing them? Do they fear impaling another person as they try to open the umbrella? Honestly, I think the enduring nature of this aversion has less to do with either of those points and everything to do with staying dry. Nobody wants the remnants of your trip through the rain on them or in their house. So, keep it closed—otherwise, you might even find yourself on the receiving end of the evil eye (see page 131).

Bad Luck Comes in Twins

Even if you've never watched Stanley Kubrick's *The Shining*, I'm willing to bet you recognize the scene where the uber-creepy twin girls are standing in a long hallway, asking Danny Torrance to play with them. It's an eerie and aesthetically stunning scene that has been replicated for decades, and, as original as it is, it takes advantage of the long-held belief that there's something unsettling about twins.

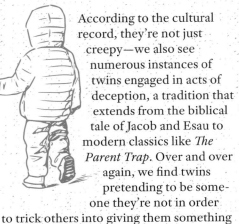

According to the cultural record, they're not just creepy—we also see numerous instances of twins engaged in acts of deception, a tradition that extends from the biblical tale of Jacob and Esau to modern classics like *The Parent Trap*. Over and over again, we find twins pretending to be someone they're not in order to trick others into giving them something they desire—for Jacob it was inheritance, for Annie and Hallie, it was a family reunion.

It's no wonder, then, that many societies believe twins to be a sign of bad luck.

Western media and literary tropes aside, the belief that twins are a bad omen has been most prominent in parts of Africa and Asia. The superstition most likely developed sometime during the Iron Age, which ranges wildly between as early as 1200 BCE to 550 BCE depending on the region. Regardless, that's well before modern medicine gave us any insight into how twins developed. In Nigeria's Igbo society, for instance, people believed that twins were sent by the gods to create chaos and destruction. As a result, twins were killed and, in some cases, left to die in order to avoid wrath from the gods.

Similarly, the shame of being born a twin in Japan was put on the mother, taken as a sign that she must have personally done something sinful to produce what was widely considered an unnatural occurrence. Sometimes the twins were killed, while other times the parents would just put one child up for adoption and keep the other over fears that the family would be cursed otherwise.

To this day, twins born in some parts of Africa and Asia continue to face stigma about being a twin. Fortunately , much of the violent and cruel treatment of twins and their families has stopped, but the misunderstandings about twins has not. If you're lucky enough to be friends with identical twins (as I am), you'll know that, unlike the movies, it's obvious which twin is which—no casually fooling friends and family in the real world.

See twins, there's no need to be sensitive—not everyone believes you're the spawn of Satan!

Lucky Rabbit's Foot

Nothing says "I'm lucky" quite like an animal's severed appendage dangling from your keychain ...

Sarcasm aside, the history of the lucky rabbit's foot is widespread, complex, problematic, and, most of all, gruesome—a far cry from the brightly-colored fur balls we see in gas stations and rest stops today. The idea that a rabbit's foot is lucky has roots in mythology from Europe, Africa, and Asia. The

Celts and Ancient Greeks believed that rabbits were considered messengers to and from the underworld because of their burrowing habits. Combine this divine connection with their speed, agility, and fertility, and rabbits seem downright supernatural— you'd be lucky to ever get your hands on one.

As it turns out, trying to find a clear origin for the lucky rabbit's foot takes just as much skill.

One theory suggests that the significance of the talisman itself can be traced back to the legend of the Br'er Rabbit, a trickster figure in traditional African folklore that took on added significance among enslaved Africans in North America, due to his ability to outwit any adversary. But the line from here to the rabbit's foot we know today is dotted at best, and there seem to be conflicting accounts on how they came to be so popular. What does seem to be consistent among origin stories, however, is that there wasn't a real push to make the charms go mainstream until the early to mid-twentieth century.

This is where the story starts to take a darker turn.

According to ads made at the time, part of what made a lucky rabbit's foot lucky was that it was caught under the "unluckiest" of circumstances: a visually impaired black person with mobility issues caught the rabbit and cut off its left foot on top of a murderer's grave on the night of Friday the 13th.

As you can likely tell, I'm tempering the language a lot here; this marketing ploy leans heavily into some extremely problematic stereotypes and beliefs about both black and disabled people. Exploiting that association to then sell trinkets to, presumably, mainly white consumers is heinous. And to (somehow) make matters worse, folklore scholars suggest that the very idea of the lucky rabbit's foot—and specifically the means of procuring it—was appropriated by white people who misinterpreted certain African American customs.

If it's any consolation, I'm pretty sure the troublesome backstories behind the rabbit's foot are not really on anyone's mind as they walk into a rest stop for some snacks and happen to see   one in a display. And for years, no real rabbits have been harmed in the making of these trinkets. Instead, they're typically a blend of latex and neon-dyed faux fur. I think it's fair to say that the exploitation of misfortune and disadvantages in order to sell some charms is also a thing of the past—at least as far as the lucky rabbit's foot goes.

Sharp Gifts Sever Ties

You're looking for a birthday gift for your best friend since elementary school. You know, the one who has the raging obsession with fantasy novels and sharp objects like swords and knives? You've never really understood the fascination with these weapons and the desire to display them all over your apartment, but you love your friend very much and want to get them something special this year. So, you think: Maybe I can get them a unique knife to add to their collection.

Well, if there's any merit to this next superstition, you might want to reconsider.

There's a superstition, most prominent in parts of Europe and North Africa, that giving your friend something sharp as a gift is a sure way to ruin your friendship. Knives in particular are considered one of the worst gifts you could give to a friend because they're loaded with bad juju and synonymous with treachery.

We see this idea expressed quite often in literature, and explicitly in the work of William Shakespeare. In *Macbeth* and *Julius Caesar*, the Bard employs knives as a means of backstabbing and betrayal. In the former play, we find Macbeth in the middle of a dilemma-induced delusion as he considers killing his king in order to seize the throne for himself. Macbeth claims to see a dagger floating before him, the blade pointed toward King Duncan's quarters and the handle ready for the taking. The dagger here represents a severing of ties from his allegiance to the king, his country, and, honestly, from reality.

Furthermore, unlike a sword, knives and daggers can be concealed. Compared to other weapons, you could easily walk up to someone and maim them with no warning and without drawing much attention to the act, which makes these weapons particularly savage—especially since you also need to be close to the person you're attacking to use a knife effectively.

Fair enough. But what if you're inclined to believe this superstition, and have no other good ideas about what to buy your friend (or the knife you've bought is nonrefundable)? The solution is shockingly simple. Just attach a coin with your gift so that your friend can give the coin back to you. This action makes the exchange a transaction, meaning it's technically no longer a gift! Sure, you'll need to explain why there's a random coin attached to the gift, and why they need to give it back to you. But now that you know the potential consequences of not including the coin, explaining this part should be a breeze!

Money on the Floor Is Money out the Door

Carrying a purse around on your night out is such a nuisance. No matter what, it feels like you can't completely relax and enjoy your evening with friends at a restaurant or bar because you must remain aware of your purse at all times. And typically, your options for relieving yourself of the burdensome purse are limited: put it on the table in front of you; put it on your lap; or keep it on the floor by your feet.

But beware: by doing the latter, you could be setting yourself up for financial ruin.

The superstition that leaving your bag or purse on the floor will hamstring your financial prospects is most common in South America and Asia, with roots in the Chinese practice of *feng shui*. To give you a quick refresher, *feng shui* is concerned with balance and the flow of energy in a space. As such, all elements of and within an environment, and where they are positioned, are extremely important to creating a happy and healthy space.

It turns out that in *feng shui*, floors are closely associated with lowliness. Think about it: we walk all over floors to get from one place to the next, and chances are you've never given them much thought unless they're very creaky or excessively dirty. As such, putting a purse full of money and other valuables on the floor is seen as a sign of disrespect toward your money and valuables, and therefore a sure way to be relieved of them.

Of course, there are also some clear, non-energy related issues with leaving your purse on the floor. The most obvious one is that it's easy to forget that you put it there and will leave without it. And I'm not a thief, but if I were, I'd probably consider targeting the bag that's been left unattended on the floor while you're chatting or dancing. But maybe I'm just proving feng shui's point. After all, you've placed your purse there and then forgotten about it. That just goes to show how little you care about the floor. It's like once your bag hits the ground, it becomes infected with whatever makes the ground so forgettable.

So, next time you're out and looking for a place to keep your purse, see if there's a coat check available that can keep it safe for you. Sure, it's a pain to pay for someone to babysit an inanimate object, but it's a small price to pay for the considerable loss that could come via a careless toss to the floor.

Lucky Penny

What's a penny worth?

Sure, it's only one cent in the United States. But if you happen to stumble upon one on your way to work or your local coffee shop, it could be worth a whole lot more than that.

Many people, especially in North America and the United Kingdom, believe that finding a penny is good luck. The Brits even consider their historic equivalent of a penny an essential good luck token for new brides. As part of the "something old, something new ..." tradition (see page 83), brides were also encouraged to put a sixpence in their shoe. And even though the sixpence no longer exists, brides in Britain still put a coin in their shoe to ensure that their newly wedded life goes off without a hitch.

The likely origin of pennies or similar small change being lucky comes from the ancient belief, which was particularly prevalent in Ancient Greece, that metal was a gift from the gods. People specifically believed that metal found on the ground was meant to be taken and kept as a talisman against evil. As metal was not only divine, but also extremely valuable, it ultimately became the primary material used for currency. Through this evolution of metal as protection to metal as currency, it's likely that the combination of ancient beliefs and waves of financial ups and downs cultivated a feeling that one needed to get their hands on all the metal they could—even if it's not worth much financially speaking.

While the United States' one-cent penny (then made of copper) was first put into circulation in 1793, the Lincoln penny we're most familiar with today wasn't put into circulation until 1909. That's an important distinction, because it plays into the other well-known part of this superstition: a penny on the ground is only lucky if it's heads up. If you pick it up when its tails up, you'll be in for some terrible luck. It's certainly not the first time the world and one's misfortunes were put strictly in black and white, and the desire to do so certainly isn't new. As with beliefs about the color black (see page 68), it's easier to put the world in a binary: things are either good or evil, lucky or unlucky. It's both comforting and devastating to think of the world in this way because it leaves no room for nuance. Growth and change are incredibly complicated; so are good and evil.

That said, I do think the straightforward nature of the lucky penny superstition is exactly why it remains so well-known and widely practiced. After all, when else in life can you be presented with a choice and know with certainty whether it's good or bad? If that penny's tails up, keep on keeping on. Heads up? Dive in with gusto! Wouldn't it be nice if all our lives involved nothing but situations that were this easy to read?

Also, I do think there is something strangely uplifting about finding a penny heads up on a busy street. It's almost like you've been singled out somehow—like you're meant to have a good day. Out of all the people out on the street, why did you find it?

He Loves Me, He Loves Me Not ...

Before Tinder or Bumble or OKCupid, people used flowers to figure out if somebody loved them.

You probably know this one from your days on the playground. You take a flower (usually just whatever was around you), think of the person you're crushing on, and start pulling the petals out as you alternate between "they love me" and "they love me not" until the very last petal is left. Whichever of the two phrases you finish on reveals how your crush feels about you. Best of all, if you didn't get the answer you wanted the first time around, you just tried again with another flower.

And again. And again.

The act is called the daisy oracle, and the lovelorn have been playing it for centuries. Some accounts say the game originally comes from France and focused on the degree to which your crush loved you: a little, a lot, madly, passionately, or not at all. It's not clear how this medieval French version of the game became binary, but what is clear is that the game has made a lasting impression on many adolescents across Europe and North America.

Today, we play this game with just about any flower we can get our hands on. But why did it all start with the daisy? Generally, daisies symbolize love and affection. In many parts of the world, they are given to new mothers. Also, since the daisy is a spring flower, their sprouting is sometimes seen as a sign of rebirth or renewal. Furthermore, daisies tend to be resilient against droughts and dry summer conditions, a heartiness that not only lends itself nicely to the turbulent arena of young love but also ensures that the daisy will be one of the most commonly available flowers for people to pick.

And, of course, the belief has endured the centuries

because love is a mystery, and we all want to know how others feel about us, even though finding out still puts you far from a workable relationship. After all, you may feel absolutely smitten with your partner of 20 years one day while the next you may wish you'd never met them at all. Neither is necessarily indicative of the relationship as a whole, and trying to navigate any partnership in such black-and-white terms can be detrimental.

But let's face it: it's a hell of a lot easier to rip petals from a daisy and call it a day than to get down to brass tacks regarding what the object of your affection thinks of you. For that reason, I don't think we'll be seeing the daisy oracle falling out of practice anytime soon.

Chain E-mails

~~*%$THIS REALLY WORKS!! FWD TO 50 PPL BY MIDNIGHT & KISS UR CRUSH!!

Whether you were on Facebook, AOL, MySpace, or even—gasp—Hotmail in the early 2000s, you probably saw hundreds of these messages in your inbox. Sometimes they were about love, sometimes about money. Occasionally, your very life was on the line.

At the end of the day, you had a choice: forward the email to a specified number of friends and family and get all the money/love/fame/fortune you've ever wanted, or ignore the message and end up alone, penniless, etc. Once you had read the message, there was no going back; you had to act. And while I do (and did) consider myself quite reasonable, these messages always got me thinking: What if?

It might seem ridiculous today that anyone would fall for such obvious spam. But you have to remember that most people in the late '90s and early aughts were just getting used to the internet and had no idea how it really worked. This lack of certainty about this thing called the World Wide Web and what it was capable of made it a perfect breeding ground for these types of messages to proliferate, preying on the hope and fear caused by the uncertainty that tends to accompany powerful new technology and ideas.

While the Internet may be relatively new, these sorts of chain letters are not. In fact, the concept of duplicating messages for positive outcomes can be traced across history all the way back to Ancient Egypt. The idea really took off, however, around the nineteenth century, following the formation of the US Post Office Department (not to be confused with the US Postal Service, which began in the 1970s). Letters ranged from sending prayers to loved ones for good luck to asking for donations. But all of them had one simple instruction: send this letter to your friends and family or you will suffer. Like the more modern chain e-mails, some of the letters included "true stories" about what happened to people who received the letter and did not forward it on, including people who died just days after having read the message and ignoring it. It's also worth noting that some of the most notorious chain letters emerged around times of great hardship and uncertainty in the United States, including during the World Wars and the Great Depression.

Which brings us back to the internet. Even today we face a constant battle for control of our lives as they become more and more entwined with the digital world. Our work, social, and love lives are almost exclusively online. We still don't know for sure how it's impacting our well-being and development, and yet it feels like we don't have the time or space to question it. In the absence of understanding, it's natural to try and make something meaningful out of nothing, as this meaning provides control—or the illusion of it, at least. As silly as it sounds now, it makes a lot of sense that web surfers young and old were persuaded into believing that these messages really held hidden powers if you didn't follow through on their commands.

But I still haven't been kissed by my crush, so maybe they were real.

The Color Black

You've probably already picked up on a pattern: black is a particularly unlucky color. Between black cats, black sheep, and crows, people have developed an aversion to the color in many parts of the world, but especially in Europe and North America. And indeed, black continues to elicit images of death, depression, and doom.

The link between black and things seen as taboo is as simple as night and day— literally. Through centuries of storytelling and religious domination, people have sought to make the differentiation of "good" and "bad" as clear as possible. Because nighttime is obviously dark due to of the lack of sunlight, black has become the stand-in for the things that nighttime has historically represented: debauchery, witchcraft, and wickedness. White, on the other hand, has been linked closely to the light of day, and therefore to purity, morality, and overall goodness. But these associations reached well beyond the page. The connection between black and wickedness was used to perpetuate racist stereotypes against people with darker skin compared to most Europeans. And these tropes continue to unconsciously drive racism to this day.

Not every culture associates the color black with all things terrible, however. In China, black is associated with water, suggesting vastness and depth. Black can also be linked to wisdom and intelligence. In a similar vein, Goth subcultures have embraced the darkness and have created a global community around taboo concepts like death, dying, and the occult, and often express themselves through black clothing and makeup.

Personally, I think black encourages thought and reflection. It's deeply alluring and, quite frankly, immediately makes any outfit look 10 times cooler.

Then again, I do tend to be a bit morbid.

An Acorn a Day Keeps the Doctor Away

Money doesn't grow on trees—especially now with the rise of cryptocurrency, which research has shown actually kills trees. However, there's a belief in England that safety and well-being do grow on trees, in the form of acorns.

To get to the root of this lucky charm's origins, it's important to know that England's national tree is the

English Oak, which produces these little nuts in abundance. Nicknamed "fruit of the oak," acorns were seen as small, unassuming tokens that carry the power and strength of the oak in a much tinier package.

But there's also a bit of magic embedded in this superstition. For many years, acorns were considered magical because they could produce massive trees from such a small seed, which seemed impossible without the help of a little enchantment. Additionally, witches in the early seventeenth century would pass acorns as a way of assuring each other that they were safe to be around. As this was right around the time the Christian church was focused on persecuting potential witches for their beliefs, it was imperative that a practitioner was certain it was safe before expressing their beliefs.

Eventually, acorns evolved from being a token of safety, solidarity, and strength to good luck charms that promoted health and well-being. It seems that this development was powered by several anecdotes from English soldiers and sailors who claimed that carrying an acorn on their person saved them from certain death, testaments that have kept the belief in lucky acorns strong to this day.

And it makes sense. At some level, we all want to believe what the acorn teaches: big things can come from small beginnings.

The Suitcase

It's safe to say that after more than two years of locking down against COVID-19, we're all feeling a little restless. Maybe you've already snuck in a tropical vacation or two since restrictions started loosening up. If so, I'm jealous.

But maybe those jaunts haven't been enough to satisfy your wanderlust and you're hoping to go on more sojourns—many more. Before you try something drastic like quitting your job to become a travel blogger, though, you might want to try this simple trick: there's a belief in parts of Central and South America that walking around the block with a suitcase at midnight on New Year's Day will give you more opportunities to travel in the coming year. The more times you go around the block, the more trips you'll take.

It's unclear exactly how or where this tradition started, but it seems to be especially popular in Colombia and Mexico and continues to be practiced throughout the Latinx diaspora.

There are some conflicting thoughts on what should be packed in the suitcase. Some people believe it doesn't have to be packed at all—an accommodating bunch, since an empty suitcase would help you run around the block many more times. Others say you should carefully curate the contents of the bag to match what you'd take on your potential excursion. So, if you're hoping to hit the beach, skip the extra parka and mittens that could come in handy on your mid-winter walk, and opt for your shorts and swimsuit.

Personally, this is a New Year's ritual I can finally get behind. Anything to increase the odds of travel is great, obviously. But I love that, unlike the kiss at midnight and setting of resolutions, this belief is fueled by hope rather than pressure and expectations. After all, it sucks to be the only person at a party who doesn't have someone to kiss when the clock strikes 12, even if you're happily single or just not interested in general. And resolutions? Well, it seems to me like they're just another excuse to beat yourself up for simply being human and having off days.

Best of all, if your circuit around the block doesn't lead to any trips, that just might mean you're right where you were meant to be all along.

Why'd You Leave the Keys up on The Table?

When I first discovered that, in Sweden, it's bad luck to leave your keys on a table, all I could think about was "Chop Suey!"

It's not Swedish, but it's one of my favorite System of a Down songs, and I could not get it out of my head as I was looking into the background of this belief. Not the worst earworm to have crawling through one's head, if you ask me, and it proved to be surprisingly helpful in thinking about what this "keys on the table" superstition means.

So, what do the Swedes see as problematic about leaving your keys on the table? Besides the potential pitfalls of giving them a chance to get lost in the sea of other placeless objects that inevitably crowd a tabletop, it's not entirely clear how keys left on a table will lead to a string of misfortunes—it seems to be just "one of those things." But, in the absence of a clear origin, there is at least a story. And it's somewhat controversial.

Back in the nineteenth century, it was allegedly customary for sex workers in Sweden to indicate their availability to potential clients by leaving their keys beside them on a table. Once this system made its way to the masses, it suddenly behooved people to avoid leaving their keys on the table (presumably in public), lest they be confused for a sex worker. How did wanting to avoid this misunderstanding turn into something that could turn the Fates against you?

One theory is that, instead of telling people—particularly children—that they shouldn't leave keys on the table because it made them look like a prostitute, it was easier and more palatable for everyone involved to simply say it would lead to bad luck.

I mentioned earlier that this origin story is controversial, as there are many Swedes who argue that this theory is completely made up and that the true origin has far more to do with everyday life. One obvious theory is that leaving keys on a table makes losing them more likely, and losing your keys means you could get locked out of your own house. Bad luck, indeed. Another theory is that the superstition was inspired by a similar Eastern Europe myth that leaving or dropping a key on a table means you'll go broke.

Which leads me back to "Chop Suey!" Give it a listen: I think we can all agree that death, loss, morality, and anger are the song's major themes. And with this superstition in mind, "Why'd you leave the keys up on the table? / Here you go create another fable (you wanted to)" becomes a little more meaningful. It isn't really the keys on the table that are freaking Serj Tankian out, but perhaps his own overconsumption, carelessness, and abuse that lead to the tragedy the song is concerned with. The keys tossed thoughtlessly on the table are not the cause of misfortune, but a symptom.

I can't say for sure that System of a Down was or wasn't inspired by this Swedish and Eastern

European superstition (they probably weren't), but I appreciate the added perspective it provided. And maybe from now on I'll keep my keys somewhere a little less problematic.

Lucky Cornicello

In Naples, good luck comes in the form of a charm shaped like a chile pepper.

The lucky cornicello is primarily used to ward off the evil eye (see page 131). However, this horn-shaped trinket can also be used to promote fertility (I'll give you three guesses why). The cornicello's origins as a lucky charm can be traced back to more than 3,000 years ago, when people would hang large, horn-shaped objects from their doors to attract good luck and fertility. The horns also represented power, strength, and wealth—channeling the energy that horned animals seemed to possess.

Over time, the size of these horns started to shrink. And instead of hanging them outside the house, Neapolitans began opting for charms and pendants so they could be worn on the body every day in order to get the ultimate amount of protection and ... other benefits.

Cornicello charms have historically been made of red coral and silver. Some were even made out of bone, which is itself a material that has longstanding associations with protection and vitality (see page 167). But today, the attraction to the cornicello has spread beyond Naples and many Italians across the globe wear them as gold necklaces or hang them from their car's rearview mirror.

Even though the means of donning the cornicello have changed over the years, the reasons have largely remained the same: good fortune, good health, and good sex. Sounds like a charmed life to me.

White Lighters

When well-known people pass away suddenly, the rest of us grow desperate to find a pattern that can help us make sense of what seems like a random and particularly tragic end. One of the most popular examples of this is the so-called "27 Club," which consists of extremely talented musicians like Jimi Hendrix, Janis Joplin, and Kurt Cobain, who all passed away at the age of 27.

But there's allegedly another connection found among these gone-too-soon superstars: white lighters.

The belief that white lighters are bad luck is well known among marijuana smokers, and can be linked back to a couple potential origins. The first, of course, is its connection to the 27 Club. Rumor has it that many of the artists had a white lighter in their possession at the time of their demises. However, this myth has actually been busted since BIC (one of the world's biggest producers of lighters) has stated they didn't even start producing white lighters until the 1980s, which would mean Jimi and Janis were spared. There have also been no official reports of white lighters found at these scenes, so it's not quite clear how the connection between the 27 Club and white lighters was made in the first place.

The other potential origin, however, does make some sense. If you were to use the bottom of a lighter as a tool to tamp down the weed in your pipe before you smoke it, you'd more likely than not get some residual ash on the bottom, which could out you as a user if you were ever pulled over by the cops. Furthermore, I've read some anecdotes where people insist that white lighters must be bad luck because every time someone in their company has a white lighter, the police seem to be right around the corner. That's less and less a problem today as marijuana slowly becomes decriminalized, but the power of this myth remains strong. And frankly, given all the colorful options for lighters these days, why choose a plain old white lighter anyway?

Four Is Not
the Magic Number

In some East Asian countries, it's not the number 13 that keeps people up at night. Instead, it's 4 that no one wants to see, because of how closely the word for it sounds to the word for "death" in Chinese (specifically Cantonese), Japanese, and Korean.

While death is a taboo topic in many cultures, it is considered particularly distasteful in China, meaning people will go to great lengths to avoid even getting a whiff of the concept—since even slight contact can curse you into suffering an early demise.

Much like countries with superstitions against the number 13, many people in this part of the world do what they can to avoid the number 4 whenever possible. Because drivers in China have some say over the sequence of numbers on their license plates, many choose to avoid 4 altogether, or at least try to avoid having 4 end the sequence. And in Japan, tetraphobia means that most elevators skip the 4th floor, rooms numbered 4 and 40 through 49 are typically skipped in hotels and hospitals, and giving 4 of anything to somebody is strongly discouraged. The fear is strong enough that the Japanese camera maker Fuji jumped from the series 3 to the series 5 in its production lines.

Unlike the superstition surrounding 13, however, there do not seem to be any particularly unlucky

days of the week associated with the
cursed 4. But any number containing the digit 4 can be considered
unlucky, depending on what the
other number(s) in the sequence
sound like.

What's fascinating about these various unlucky number beliefs is that there
isn't universal agreement on one single number of
doom, which I think illuminates something critical
about superstitions: good luck and misfortune are
completely subjective. What one person on one side
of the globe considers unlucky may be completely
innocuous to another person on the other side of the
globe. It doesn't necessarily mean that the superstition or belief is not true or meaningful in the context
of where it exists, but it does go to show you just
how much of an impact culture, environment, and
language have upon the development of our beliefs.

Itchy Palms

Not all itchy palms are created equal. Depending
on which of your palms is itchy, you may be about
to come into some money, or lose whatever you
already have.

The superstition that an itchy right palm is a sign
of incoming wealth and an itchy left palm signifies
future loss shows up across multiple cultures and
regions, so it is difficult to determine exactly where
it comes from. Though there does seem to be some

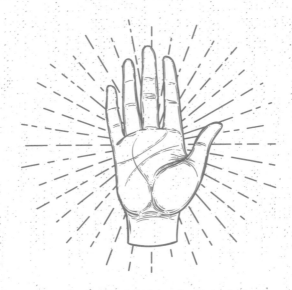

disagreement on which itchy palm is the lucky one depending on where you live, there's a surprisingly deep connection between beliefs about money and palms. In palm reading, readers will examine your "money line," which sits in the center of the hand, and is said to reveal your economic prospects. There's also the expression "to grease one's palm," which means giving someone a bribe on the sly. There's even a reference to this superstition (or at least the idea of an itchy palm being a sign of getting money) in Shakespeare's *Julius Caesar*, which was first performed right around the beginning of the seventeenth century.

So, while it seems random that we'd associate itchy

palms with money, we've actually been doing it for centuries. But why? One likely origin of the palm-to-money connection comes from the Saxons, who believed that silver was a cure for most ailments—itchy palms included. Somehow, through generations and generations of using silver as a salve, people began to believe that an itch on the hand meant some money was heading your way.

I for one would feel more confident in this superstition if we could all agree on which hand meant I was about to get money or lose money. The markets are volatile enough!

Ceremonies
& Rituals

Something Old, Something New, Something Borrowed, Something Blue

Everyone has their own take on what a wedding needs to be a success, and your wedding will be no exception. But one opinion that you might want to listen to is when someone tells you that you should have something old, something new, something borrowed, and something blue at the ceremony.

This old English belief and rhyme has been around for centuries to help people remember to have these four lucky items on hand in order to give you and your partner the best chance at a happy life together. While this collection of items ultimately began as a means of warding off the evil eye (see page 131 for more), each item in the jingle does serve a particular purpose:

"Something old" is believed to represent continuity and tradition, as well as protection for your future children. Oftentimes the item was a piece of jewelry passed down in the family, or some other kind of heirloom.

"Something new" is supposed to symbolize the life the couple will make together and is arguably the easiest item to obtain. Even something like the wedding dress or the wedding bands can check this box.

"Something borrowed" can be anything from a

happily married friend or relative and is meant to give you an extra boost in your marriage, as their good fortune will rub off on you.

And "something blue" is meant to ward off the evil eye awhile also representing love, purity, and fidelity.

While people tend to know up to "something blue," the full rhyme actually ends with "and a sixpence in your shoe." Sixpence pieces were discontinued in the United Kingdom in the 1980s, and of course they were only used in the UK to begin with. Today, any American couples familiar with the full rhyme might put a penny in their shoe instead.

The rules have changed slightly to be a little more flexible to the couple's aesthetic and sensibilities. These days, so long as these elements are incorporated into the wedding in some way (favors, invitations, etc.), you'll still reap the benefits. Who knew marital bliss was so easy!

Bless You!

On the ever-growing list of iconic duos, there's one that has managed to hold up for centuries: a sneeze and a "God bless you."

People from all corners of the world are taught from an early age that you must say "bless you" or "God bless you" (or "*Gesundheit*" for Germans and/or atheists) after someone sneezes. The response has been drilled into people so fervently that it's almost a compulsion—just sneeze in a crowded room and count the number of blessings you receive from people who otherwise would have paid you no mind. As such, I'd argue it might be the most commonly practiced superstition in the world—so much so that you might not have even realized it as a superstition until this very moment.

There are a couple of common theories regarding the origin of what has now become instinct. One idea suggests that during the Middle Ages, sneezing was an early sign that one had contracted the bubonic plague, meaning a painful, sudden death was near. In turn, people would bless the person before they succumbed. Another theory, which extends all the way back to the Ancient Romans, is that a sneeze could eject the soul from the body, so people would bless the sneezer to block any evil spirits in the area from stealing their soul.

And, while there have always been some rumors that sneezing can result in some unfortunate physiological effect—such as making your heart stop or make your eyes pop out of their sockets—science has proven there's nothing inherently harmful in a sneeze. So, fortunately, the blessing doesn't have to carry both body and soul to safety.

Whichever origin story sounds most believable to you, I think the underlying theme behind this superstition is a desire for protection from the unfathomable. Whether it's death from a deadly and incurable disease or possession by a malevolent force, we want those around us—and ourselves, in turn—to be safe from things we can't control. Though I don't believe that people who sneeze are about to die or be possessed by the devil, I do think there's a unique comfort in wishing someone well after they sneeze. Besides, though we have debunked the heart-stopping myth, and the bubonic plague is now treatable, the jury's technically still out on evil spirits possessing your body. And personally, it's not a chance I'm willing to take.

Cross Your Fingers

Have an interview for a super cool job? Cross your fingers! Walking under a ladder? Cross your fingers! Did you just see your friend's new band play for the first time and now they're asking you how it was? Tell them it was great and (discreetly) cross your fingers!

Crossing your fingers—or more specifically, looping your middle finger around your index finger—is such a well-known superstition that there's even an emoji for it. While the act is most often portrayed as a way to attract luck to yourself or others, crossing your fingers is surprisingly versatile. In addition to attracting luck, you can also use it to deflect bad luck—like when you have no choice but to walk under a ladder (see page 49)—and to protect yourself when you tell a lie.

This superstition is most common in North America and the United Kingdom, and most likely has its roots in Christianity. After all, crossing your fingers in any of the situations mentioned above is essentially like calling upon a higher power for aid. One theory regarding its origin suggests that early followers of Christianity, which at the time was banned throughout the Roman Empire, would greet each other with secret hand signals. One of these signals involved forming a cross with the fingers to let someone know that they were in safe company.

Once Christianity became more established and secret signals were no longer necessary, the act of crossing fingers became a way for two people to make a wish come true, and then evolved into a solo undertaking sometime in the fourteenth century. And, of course, somewhere between then and today, crossing your fingers evolved even further to be less religiously loaded while somehow still holding much of the same significance—especially if you're crossing your fingers in the middle of a lie.

No Cheers with Water

Making a toast with water is considered so unlucky that it's even banned by the US military.

According to the US Navy's "Mess Night Manual," which painstakingly outlines the proper etiquette and pro- cedures for special events, "toasts are never drunk with liqueurs, soft drinks, or water. Tradition is that the object of a toast with water will die by drowning."

The Navy isn't the only group that believes in this superstition, as its inception far precedes the conception of the United States itself. This myth originates from Ancient Greece, where toasting with water was actually a common custom meant to cele- brate the dead and send a loved one who had passed off to the underworld. The water represented water from the river Lethe, which the recently deceased would drink from in order to forget their lives in the living world.

Because of the nature of this custom, making a toast with water in any other context was akin to wishing the subject of the toast—or even yourself—dead. Additionally, because a toast was also considered an offering to the gods, a glass of water, with its flavor- lessness and mundane character, was considered an insult and could therefore subject you to bad luck in the future.

Today, this superstition has gone far beyond the

Greeks, and is an inviolable part of toasting etiquette throughout Europe and North America. It's considered so unlucky to cheers with water that people say it's better to toast with an empty glass. Teetotalers out there, take note.

Rain on Your Wedding Day

It's not ironic, but it is considered lucky.

The belief that a rainy wedding day is a sign of good luck most likely comes from deep-rooted beliefs about water serving as a symbol of life, renewal, growth, and unity with the divine. In Hinduism, for instance, rain is considered an offering from the gods.

As if that wasn't enough, another theory behind this superstition suggests that rain provides the newly wedded couple a clean slate—a sort of physical manifestation of their new life together. Yet another is that rain during a wedding provides a stronger bond, literally. This particular belief is rooted in the practice of traditional Celtic handfasting ceremonies, where the couple's hands are literally tied together, (hence the idiom "tying the knot"). Since wet rope is more difficult to untie, people saw it as a sign that the relationship would always hold together.

Frankly though, I think there's a much more straight-forward reason why exchanging your vows in the rain is such a good omen for marriage. A traditional North American wedding costs thousands of dollars and takes anywhere from months to years of planning. Having the weather not cooperate on the day that most likely took years and thousands of dollars to put together can be frustrating, to say the least, and it's also your first big test as a married couple. If you both can remain mindful of the reason for the occasion and refuse to let the storm wash away your joy, that's a very good sign for the prospects of your marriage, and for your life together in general.

So, if you have a wedding coming up and see rain in the forecast, don't fret—it might be the best thing that ever happened to you and your beloved.

Make a Wish

You're sitting at the head of a table, surrounded by friends and family. Suddenly, the lights in the room go out, and you're in total darkness. You hear the subtle strike of a match from the kitchen. The smell of sulfur wafts your way, and slowly, a soft glow grows brighter and brighter as your mom makes her way to the dining room. She begins to sing. They all do. Happy Birthday to you!

That glow coming your way is the dozens of candles burning atop your favorite cake, the one that only your mother truly knows how to make. One candle for each year of life. As the singing continues, the blazing confection draws closer and closer, until your mother places the cake right in front of you. You gaze upon it. The candles are melting quickly, dripping vibrantly colored wax all over the frosting.

Suddenly, the singing stops. You know what you must do.

You close your eyes, make a wish, and take one big breath in.

And then, with all your might, you breathe out to extinguish the flames and save your cake from its waxy doom.

Your friends and family cheer your valiant effort and incredible lung capacity! In this beautiful, happy moment, your wish seems well within reach.

Blowing out candles on your birthday has been a time-honored tradition in Europe and North America for centuries, and the practice has now spread to cultures around the world. The ritual can be traced back to Ancient Greece, where people would bring small round cakes with them on visits to the temples of Artemis, goddess of the moon. These cakes were adorned with lit candles to symbolize the lunar glow, and the Greeks believed that when the candles were blown out, the resulting smoke not only carried your prayers up to the gods, it also helped ward off evil spirits.

So how did we get from blowing out candles as a means of worship to making birthday wishes? First, we can thank the Ancient Egyptians for the concept of a birthday celebration, which is based on the coronation celebrations of the pharaohs. Kinderfeste, a centuries-old German tradition where kids were presented a cake studded with lit candles, was another major influence—if the children could extinguish all of the candles in one breath, they would be granted a wish.

And so, the birthday wish was born.

The idea that each year, once a year, you have a moment to take stock of the things you have and the things you want in life is magical. Whether or not you believe that making a birthday wish will lead to that wish coming true, it's hard to resist the feeling that maybe, just maybe, something incredible will happen this year. Just be sure to keep it to yourself, if it does.

Sit Before You Go

Your flight is supposed to depart in two hours and you're still running around trying to get ready. Between wrapping up everything at work, shopping for last minute toiletries, and packing, you're just now at the point you can arrange your ride. Your stress is through the roof. You seriously need to get

out of here and go on this
vacation ...

But before you leave, make
sure to take a moment to sit
in silent contemplation.
It may be just what you
need to make the rest of
your trip a breeze.

Many people in
Ukraine, Russia,
and other Eastern
European countries
are adamant about mak-
ing sure they and everyone else going along on the
trip take at least a few seconds to sit in silence before
they head out. Whether it's for vacation or business,
by plane or by car, any period of longer-than-usual
travel must begin with a moment of silence.

One theory about the origin of this superstition
points to the ancient belief that the home is full of
spirits that protect the household and its residents
from evil. Taking a moment of silence, therefore, is
considered an act of recognition and gratitude for
the spirits and their continued efforts to protect your
home.

But there's also a very practical, Zen element to this
superstition. Taking a moment to just sit quietly
before rushing out the door gives you a minute to
think about what you're taking with you and what
you may be missing. According to some believers,

this brief respite provides the spirits are opportunity to tell you that you're not quite ready to leave the house yet.

On an admittedly sentimental note, there's something quite touching about taking a moment to reflect and appreciate what we have. If we've learned anything from the COVID-19 pandemic, it's that the world and our individual lives can change drastically in a matter of days. When we sit in silent appreciation of our "home," we're acknowledging the peace it provides, how fortunate we are, and how this feeling may never be replicated.

Whether you feel the need to appease the house spirits or you just want to give yourself a moment to process before you head out the door, this little ritual might be something you'll want to add to your to pre-travel to-do list. After all, there's no telling what crucial realizations these moments could provide.

Over the Threshold

The world of superstitions is no stranger to misogyny. If you've read at least a few of these entries, I'm sure you've noticed how many superstitions and rituals were meant to stifle or control women under the guise of protecting them. Certainly not all of them, but an unsettling amount.

Heads up, gents: carrying a bride over the threshold just so happens to be one of these outdated and sexist superstitions. Ye be warned.

There are several possible origins of this time-hon-ored practice. The tamest of the bunch has to do with the couple protecting themselves from evil spirits. Closely tied to the Eastern European super-stition of not greeting people over a threshold (see page 119), many cultures used to believe that spirits resided in the threshold of a household. Working under that logic, carrying the bride through the doorway made it harder for spirits to possess her, and the newlywed couple would live happily ever after. A variation of this particular theory is that if the bride, in her long dress and ornamental shoes, tripped on the threshold, she would anger the spirits there and place the new union in peril. Having the groom carry the bride through the doorway elimi-nated this possibility.

Not too bad, right? Well, here's where things get a little dark. Another potential origin of this tradition comes from medieval Europe, where women were expected to appear unenthused about getting mar-ried. Therefore, the groom would pick up the "hesi-tant" bride as if bringing her into his life by force.

Today, people continue this ritual not out of fear or out of a desire to strongarm someone into a union, but simply because it's been around for so long it has become ingrained in Western wedding traditions.

To be fair, many couples now skip the act entirely and decide to step over the threshold together to show that they are equal partners in their new life. I like that. But knowing what I know now, I think I'll just skip the threshold part altogether if I ever get married.

The Lucky Chimney Sweep

You've been planning your wedding for months and, finally, everything seems to be in the right place. You've got the seating arrangements locked in, you've got the band, the caterer, the florist, the venue, and the photographer all lined up. All that's left now is ... making sure the chimney sweep's going to show?

That's right: those soot-covered gents with the hats and long brooms over their shoulders. While they spend their days going in and out of chimneys making sure there's no buildup that could release toxic fumes into your house or cause it to burn down, it turns out they also offer blessings to the bride and groom. And without one at the wedding, your odds of marital bliss may be slim.

The presence of the chimney sweep has been a tradition at English weddings for centuries, even though the reason behind it is shrouded in mystery. One story claims that the custom started with King George II, whose horse got spooked during the royal procession. Fortunately for everyone there, a chimney sweep swooped in to calm the horse before it could ruin the event. Though the ceremony's savior disappeared before the king had a chance to thank him, George was so grateful that he gave chimney sweeps everywhere the royal blessing.

It's worth noting that King George II, while a decent enough ruler, tended to doubt himself, and would frequently seek guidance in various signs and symbols. So, though it seems bizarre for a king to make such a declaration off of just one moment, there seems to be some history of George leaping to wild conclusions based on a bit of auspiciousness crossing his path.

There has also been speculation that the chimney sweep is good luck at weddings because of the connection between the color of soot and fertility, as black, while most often and immediately associated with death and doom, can also symbolize fertility and wisdom in some cases (see page 68).

I'd like to propose my own theory based on almost no real-life evidence at all: maybe chimney sweeps are just pleasant people to be around. If they're anything like Bert from *Mary Poppins*, you'll have someone who can take the dancefloor to the next level. Bert, if you're available, and if I ever get married, you're totally invited!

So, if you're looking for a happy, long-lasting marriage, let the chimney sweep drop in and shake the groom's hand, kiss the bride, and spread good tidings—after all, a little soot never hurt anybody, but divorce certainly has.

Early Birthdays

Every year is an accomplishment. Between pandemics, extreme weather events, and the ever-looming possibility of some sort of freak accident, it really is a miracle that you've survived yet another trip around the sun. And yet, here you are. So, you count down the months before the big day, then the weeks, then the days. And then finally, one day to go. You've waited a whole 364 days just for this moment. It's so close you can already taste that birthday cake.

You want so badly to just start this darn celebration. You think to yourself: What's the harm in celebrating just one day early?

In parts of Europe and Asia, you'd be much better off waiting that one more day ... assuming you even live that long.

People in countries like Germany and India believe that celebrating your birthday early—or even just wishing someone a happy birthday before the actual day—is bad luck. If anything, you should celebrate late. In fact, some particularly paranoid Germans allegedly won't celebrate their birthdays until the day after, just to be safe.

In India, the bad luck comes from the hubris of celebrating early. In doing so, you're saying that you absolutely will turn a year older, even though you've not yet done so. In reality, anything could happen to us at any moment; no tomorrow, not even your birthday, is guaranteed. So celebrating your birthday (or any holiday for that matter) before the actual day is definitely tempting fate.

Obviously, there are practical reasons why you might want to celebrate your birthday on a different day. If you're planning a party and your birthday happens to fall on a weekday, you're most likely going to plan the event for a weekend so you and your friends don't have to worry about work or school the next day. That's fine. Just make sure it's for the weekend after the actual day so you're not setting yourself up for a bad time. Be patient and celebrate the moment in which you're currently alive rather than jumping ahead to a day that may or may not come—even if it's only a day away. You never know what could happen.

On the
Home Front

Wrong Side of the Bed

Everybody has those days where nothing seems to be going right. You're tired, you're in a bad mood, you're constantly running late, you forgot your lunch in the fridge, you spilled your coffee on the way to the office (see page 171 for more on this incident). The mistakes just keep piling up, and everyone and everything is grating. You're miserable and you want others to feel your misery, too. Some might say you woke up on the wrong side of the bed. Is it possible you actually did?

This common phrase is based on a superstition that dates back to the Roman Empire. Since the Latin word for "left" is *sinister*, Romans thought it was bad luck to sleep on the left side of the bed or to exit it on that side. Do so, and you're putting your whole day in peril.

Today, waking up on the wrong side of the bed is just an expression, but if one wanted to be literal about, I think there is a path that gets you there. Say you were restless during the night, tossing and turning, constantly changing where you laid your head. Maybe you ended up on the side of the bed that you don't normally sleep on. And, in your dazed rush to get to work after hitting the snooze button one too many times, you get up on the side that is closest. Unfortunate events pile up throughout the day, you grow increasingly incensed, and while it doesn't have anything to do with the side of the bed you got up on, it also kind of does, right?

What's in a Sneeze?

Sure, a sneeze could mean you're catching a cold or suffering from allergies (my condolences). But assuming you're not falling ill or experiencing an allergic reaction, a random sneeze might not be so random after all.

Many people around the world believe that a sneeze is a sign you're on somebody's mind. There are several variations of this snot-related superstition. In Poland, sneezing is believed to be an indicator that your mother-in-law is speaking poorly of you. Many East Asian cultures believe that both the number of sneezes and their intensity give you extra insight into who is talking about you and why. For example, one loud sneeze means someone is praising you. Two sneezes, however, means someone is talking trash. Should that twofer be followed by another sneeze, you can assume that the person who is talking about you is in love with you.

As mentioned on page 84, civilizations through-out human history have seen a strong connection between this involuntary bodily function and the soul. And, in a roundabout way, you could even suggest that this superstition is yet another means of protecting your soul. Uncertainty over how people view us and the accompanying anxiety can be overwhelming. Feeling as though your body can alert you to what's going on and where you stand can undoubtedly be soothing. On the other hand, it's possible that knowing someone is talking about you but not being totally sure who is doing it or what it's about might be worse—sort of like knowing the exact date of your death and not being able to do anything about it.

Regardless of how you feel about gossip in general, I think it's worth questioning what a "positive" or "negative" comment is. Is it simply trash talking, or is it a valid criticism that you simply don't want to face? Is the praise over things you value? If it isn't, is it still something you should put stock in?

Still, there's a strange comfort in making meaning out of something random and innocuous. And the idea that someone is thinking of us at any given point in our daily lives—whether good or bad—can make us feel less alone. Let's just hope that "someone" isn't the Grim Reaper.

Split the Pole

Between trash cans, mailboxes, telephone poles, and plodding people, walking down the street hand-in-hand with someone can be a challenge, frequently feeling as though the world's working against your unity. Sometimes, you both have to separate for a moment to get around an obstacle. But beware— doing so could make the split permanent.

Walking around a pole or person in your way by momentarily parting with your partner—also known as "splitting the pole"—is considered extremely bad luck, and a sign that your relationship is destined to come to an end. The belief seems to be most common in North America, particularly in the South. There are also variations to this superstition—some people believe that the younger person in the pair will get the brunt of the misfortune if a pole is split, as that younger person is suddenly cut off from the wisdom of the older person.

Another superstition stemming from this one is that you can reverse the curse by saying "bread and butter" aloud while splitting the pole. Some believe that only one person needs to say it upon separation, while others hold that both people must say it at the exact same time or the shield won't stick. Still others think that anyone who believes a simple phrase can ward off the heap of bad luck that splitting the pole creates is kidding themselves.

While the origins of this myth remain a mystery, I think we can find some answers just by looking at it in context. Let's say the pair in question is a child and a guardian (parent, grandparent, etc.). There's an extremely practical reason why you—as an adult—wouldn't want to be separated from the child, so I can imagine a situation in which adults turned this very real safety concern into a myth that could scare kids into not wanting to get separated. As we know, a desire to deter unsafe behavior and gain control is fertile ground for superstitions to grow. Sure, you might be a rebellious kid, but nobody wants a streak of bad luck.

As far as romantic couples go, I can see this story being a way for lovers to quell their anxieties about their loved one going astray and finding someone else. If you're always holding hands, nobody will get any ideas about potential availability, and neither person in the relationship can wander off with someone else. But if that's a concern, sounds like there are bigger problems in the relationship beyond splitting the pole.

Step on a Crack, Break Your Mama's Back

Yeah, that's a direct quote from Devo's "Whip It." But it's also a common superstition, and one that I admit I follow closely. You just never know, you know?

The origin of this superstition is tough to pin down. Though I will say that I, and apparently most people in North America, first heard this sinister little rhyme at recess in grade school, where it wasn't unusual to see groups of children hopping around in dramatic fashion to avoid cracks in the pavement. Of course, there were always a few kids that would emphatically stomp on these cracks with little care for the state of their mothers' backs, but any analysis of that is far above my pay grade.

While a source beyond the playground is difficult to track down, it's clear that the idea behind this superstition preys upon a fundamental fear of youth: something terrible happening to one of your care-givers. It could also very well be a caregiver's way of relieving their own fears of something happening to a child by making them more alert and aware of their surroundings. After all, stepping on a big enough crack could make you trip and fall—maybe even break your own back. But since kids often struggle envisioning the consequences their actions may have for themselves, maybe it was more effective to place the effects of their actions on their unwitting mother, as it's safe to say that most children would hate to see their mothers in pain, especially due to something they did.

Pretty tricky. But hey, me and millions of others have shown that it's plenty effective.

Yellow Ain't Mellow

Picture a table draped in a white tablecloth and, in the center, a vase of brilliant yellow flowers—so yellow they seem to reflect all of the light streaming through the windows, giving your otherwise drab kitchen a warm, loving glow. The glow is especially brilliant because your partner just brought them home moments ago, surprising you with a spontaneous trip to the florist on their way back from your favorite café. Between the rich smell of espresso floating through the room and those vibrant flowers, you couldn't feel luckier, or more in love.

Most people would probably agree—getting a bouquet of sunny yellow flowers from a loved one is a sweet gesture. And that (most likely) is the intention ... unless you or they happen to be from Russia.

There's a superstition in that country that receiving yellow flowers from a romantic partner is terrible luck, guaranteed to lead to arguments and, ultimately, the end of the relationship. It's also sometimes considered a sign that your partner has been unfaithful. Hence the arguments, I suppose. This superstition is so ingrained in Russian culture that it's even made its way onto the radio. Russian pop singer Natasha

Korolyova's "Yellow Tulips" tells the story of a young woman who sees her relationship with her boyfriend crumble before her eyes after he gives her a bouquet of yellow tulips. Did he do it on purpose, to signal that all was not well in the relationship? Or did he do so out of kindness, ignorant of this longstanding cultural belief, and now she's reading into things too much? Ultimately, it didn't matter—the relationship was DOA.

In general, yellow is a bit of a complicated color in Russian culture. While there are certainly some cases in which the color lives up to its sunny reputation, it's mostly associated with shades of danger and despair. *Жёлтый дом*, or "yellow house," is a derogatory term for having someone committed, inspired by an infamous yellow St. Petersburg hospital with a psych ward. There's also an association between yellow and sensationalist media—the equivalent of "yellow journalism" in English. The subtext beneath these examples is that, in addition to the cheerful connotations it carries, yellow is also connected with delusion, drama, and lies—a trio that would certainly sink any romantic relationship.

So, if you're looking for a way to show your love and loyalty to your Russian love, stick with red roses. And if you're extra superstitious, make sure you don't stick them with a bouquet featuring an even number of flowers, or you could be setting yourself up for a whole new problem (see page 46).

Curse of the Boyfriend Sweater

If you're at all familiar with relationship psychology, you're probably familiar with the concept of love languages. For instance, some people like to show their affection by giving gifts. The crafty ones among us may be more inclined to make something for our beloved, like a hat or a scarf. Just resist the urge to make a sweater. That is, if you want your relationship to have any chance of survival.

Known as the curse of the boyfriend sweater, this superstition is legendary in knitting communities, where it is believed that lovingly crafting a beautiful and cozy sweater for your partner most likely means curtains for the relationship.

Sounds ridiculous, right? How could someone be anything but charmed by a gift like that? Well, unlike many of the superstitions I've encountered in researching this book, there are quite a few anecdotes to support it being true. Ask any seasoned knitter—they'll likely know someone who experienced a surprising and painful breakup because they decided to make a sweater. Some knitters have even experienced it themselves! They had knitted items for their partner before, but a single sweater severed the bond.

So, what exactly is the culprit behind this curse? Well, people who knit, though they very much believe sweaters are jinxed, seem to dismiss the

notion of any supernatural element—no genies or malevolent fairies are hiding in the yarn, waiting to be made into a sweater so they can wreak havoc. Instead, it seems that this enduring belief comes down to basic psychology.

Knitting a sweater takes a good deal of time, resources, and commitment—not unlike a relationship. It's very possible that, in the act of sitting down and making such an elaborate gift for your loved one, you begin to think more deeply about the relationship. You see right before your eyes the time and effort you're putting into the relationship, but what about them? Are they as committed to the relationship as you are? Would they take the time to knit you a sweater? Aided by the flow of creation, such questions about the true nature of the relationship are likely to come to the surface.

There's no sweater curse for married couples, though, so if you live in a drafty old Victorian and you're eager to give your beloved a sweater to stay warm, wait until you tie the knot.

No Clipping Nails at Night

When do you usually clip your nails? If your answer is "at night," you might want to revise your schedule.

Of course, this widespread belief can be traced back to a time when the fancy and relatively foolproof nail clippers we have around the house today did not exist. People would usually just use a standard knife to clip their nails, so I think you can do the math: deadly sharp implement, low light, close to body. This terrifying trio no doubt provided the basis of the advisory against nocturnal nail cutting in many countries.

In Japan, however, they take the superstition one step further: many people in the country believe that cutting your nails at night will have catastrophic spiritual consequences. Apparently, the act opens up a few possibilities. Some say that cutting your nails at night creates portals for malevolent spirits to enter your body and possess you. Others say that your soul resides in your nails, and a nocturnal trim summons the ultimate spirit: Death itself.

This superstition reminds me of a Japanese novel by Yōko Ogawa called *The Memory Police*. It's about a society in which the entire population of an island slowly has its memory systematically erased by the local government. There are, however, a few outliers who seem unaffected by the government's methods of control and are therefore disappeared themselves. In one scene, the narrator, who is losing her memory along with the rest of the island, tries to help a friend and his family escape from being detained by the Memory Police because of their inability to forget. It's the middle of the night, and the mother asks for the narrator's help with clipping her young son's nails as they wait for their point of contact to help them escape. The narrator carefully describes the sight of the flimsy little crescents of the child's nails floating to the ground, a moment where everything else seems to be frozen. But in the blink of an eye (or seemingly so), the family suddenly vanishes, as if they had never been there at all. Did they escape, were they detained, or were they whisked away into the spirit world as punishment for this nail-related misstep? We never find out for sure.

While the cutting of nails doesn't lead to a traditional possession in this scene, within the context of the novel, it does create the conditions for an unsettling loss of identity, which is essentially what possession is.

But frankly, this superstition had me at sharp objects near appendages in low light.

Sweep You on Your Feet

Sure, you may have been swept off your feet by the vegan musician who planned a moonlight picnic on your first date. But if you want to have any chance of that relationship going further, stay away from anyone sweeping around your feet—otherwise, that romance, and every other one you get involved in, might be doomed.

The superstition that someone sweeping under your feet or accidentally brushing your feet with a broom will make you chronically single can be found in many different cultures, spanning from

Central America to Europe and the Middle East. The belief is mostly centered around young women and their ability to wed, which has historically played in important role in both a young woman's—and by default her family's—future prospects. So it makes sense that anything that could be perceived as potentially besmirching her good name would be considered bad luck and avoided at all costs.

But why would a broom be the instrument of besmirchment? While it may seem completely random, there's actually quite a bit of lore surrounding brooms and the act of sweeping. Of course, brooms are often associated with witchcraft and, in turn ... some other things. The first-known image of a witch riding a broom was drawn in the fifteenth century and was meant to show that witches had subverted their femininity—the broom had become a symbol of domesticity and femininity, since cleaning was (is) considered women's work.

And yet, despite its association with femininity, brooms are also obviously phallic. So, the salacious image of a femininity-rejecting woman (often depicted naked) riding a broomstick ... well, need I say more?

Perhaps it's a stretch, but I think it's possible that the link between broomsticks and both literal and metaphorical filth gave birth to this spinster-related superstition. We can also pull bits and pieces from other superstitions that claim sweeping near people can rid them of their good luck. And, leaning further into the gender role component, it's possible that the superstition stands as a threat to young women who are unmotivated to clean, since after all, cleaning is their responsibility. If someone is able to sweep around your feet, it means that you as the young woman are not doing your job, and therefore will not make for a suitable wife for anyone.

It's speculative, I admit. But sometimes, that's all you have. And in a world where women are still seen as lesser than in most places, it's more than enough.

These Boots Are Made for Walking (Right out of This Relationship)

Apparently, a handmade sweater isn't the only gift you should avoid giving your partner if you want things to last (see page 109). Many people across the globe believe it's bad luck to buy your beau a pair of shoes because ... well, they'll use them to walk right out of your life.

There are some slight variations to this myth depending on where you live. In Korea, it's possible to counteract the curse by offering a small token like a quarter to the gift-giver, transforming the exchange into a transaction. Any exchange, no matter how small, seems to set things right, at least in the world of superstitions.

As with so many wide-spread superstitions, it's tough to find the reason it initially took hold. Perhaps it has something to do with the lowly position shoes occupy, a gift that may signal you don't think highly of the person. Perhaps your partner is on the fence about how serious they want to be with you; a costly pair of shoes tips them over the edge, and they decide they're not ready or interested in being with you forever.

Maybe it has something to do with people's habit of removing their shoes before entering a house, a practice that implies shoes are for going—not staying. In this light, giving your partner shoes is begging them to leave the house, because it's the only way they can enjoy the gift.

In that case, let's stick to something that will keep them safe and sound and happily beside you at home—books! I've personally always been a fan of giving and receiving books as gifts. There's also that famous John Waters quote: "If you go home with somebody and they don't have books..."

I'm trying to keep this book PG-13, so if you don't know the rest, I suggest you look it up yourself. He has quite a few quotes about books, actually. The bottom line is, though, that there's nothing like a good book to kindle a memorable romance. Clearly, the same can't be said about shoes.

Upside Down Shoe

If you're like me, you probably just toss your shoes in the closet or the mudroom when you're done wearing them for the day. They might land nowhere near each other, making tracking them down the next day harder than it should be. But who cares? The important thing is that they are off my feet! In some parts of the world, however, I'd be careful about placing them, because shoes lying upside down—that is, with the soles facing up—is considered terribly unlucky.

This myth is most prominent throughout the Middle East and North Africa, where improperly arranged shoes can be incredibly insulting. Remember when President George W. Bush was giving a press conference in Iraq and an Iraqi journalist got upset, took both of his shoes off, and proceeded to hurl them at the former president? The full impact of this move was most likely lost on most people in the United States, who likely briefly chuckled and moved on, impressed that Bush was agile enough to dodge both projectiles. But rest assured, Iraqis knew that the journalist's action showed great disrespect and rebellion.

All of that is to show the significance shoes hold in Middle Eastern, North African, and even Southwest Asian cultures. The bottom of the shoe—you know, the part that traipses through all sorts of crud on a daily basis—is considered particularly offensive. If that sole is facing upward, people believe that you are showing disrespect to God, and could therefore be a victim of his wrath.

In India, a shoe with its sole up is said to lead to family conflict. This iteration of the superstition seems a bit like a "chicken or the egg" situation: Is it the upside-down shoe that leads to arguments, and therefore became a sign of bad luck; or is the sole-side-up superstition so powerful that simply seeing it gets people fearful of the dreadful things that will ensue, increasing the odds of an argument?

In some superstitious households, it might be a question worth leaving unanswered.

No Sweeping at Night

Your friend left your house hours ago, but the remnants of their stay are all over the floor. The crumbs, the sand from their shoes. You had a great time together—you always do—but this mess is killing you!

The urge to sweep up becomes more and more powerful as the night proceeds. You're tidy—but you're also superstitious, and you know you need to resist this temptation until the sun comes up. Otherwise, you'll sweep away any good luck you have.

The superstition that sweeping at night is bad luck is a widespread one and powerfully influenced by the nearly universal apprehension around nighttime.

Many cultures believe that night is when the invisible barrier between the living world and the supernatural world is at its most permeable, meaning encounters with ghosts, spirits, or evil forces are more likely. The thinking behind this particular belief is that sweeping at night will disturb the house spirits guarding your home, leaving you vulnerable to an infiltration of malevolent entities.

But there is also a perfectly rational explanation as to why you might not want to sweep at night. Remember, electricity is a relatively new phenomenon. Many of the superstitions based around avoiding certain activities at night originate from times when there was no electricity, which meant that most chores or activities were useless or downright dangerous to try to do in the middle of the night. While sweeping in low light is not necessarily physically perilous (unless you're super clumsy), one theory is that you may be sweeping away valuable items that happened to fall on the floor, like money or even family heirlooms. As a result, some people have tweaked the myth to account for this possibility, claiming a night sweep means financial hardships are around the corner.

Yes, your fastidiousness is admirable. But rules are rules. Take a load off. That mess will keep until the morning.

Not on the Threshold!

Stay away from thresholds if you're welcoming a guest into your home.

There's a superstition in parts of Eastern Europe, particularly in Russia and Poland, that greeting someone within a threshold is bad luck, and could lead to an argument. Whether your preferred welcome is a solid handshake, a hug, or a kiss, make sure to bring your guest all the way inside the house, or take a step outside of the house, before you exchange greetings.

This superstition, which still holds plenty of sway, stems from the belief that spirits reside in the threshold of every home. It's unclear exactly how this belief came to be, and why these spirits would linger in the doorway, but, if we take a step back away from the spiritual side of things, the superstition does make some sense.

After all, the purpose of a threshold is to keep anything that is outside or foreign from coming in, whether that be water and wind or bugs and rats. In these instances, the threshold provides safety and protection against potential damage. Therefore, when you enter the threshold to greet someone, it's almost as though you are taking on its function of expelling that which does not belong in your home— in essence, you have branded your guest as vermin. Obviously, this kind of alienation would cause a rift in any relationship. OK, maybe it's a bit of a leap on my part, but it does make some sense.

Also, let's not overlook the fact that trying to give someone a hug or kiss in an entranceway is just awkward. Picture it now: Doesn't it feel forced and stiff and slightly cramped, the opposite of the warm welcome you want to give someone?

At the end of the day, this belief seems to be focused on fostering good manners as a host and making others feel welcome—two things that always seem to be in danger of disappearing. Maybe etiquette is just superstition in disguise.

Ugly Babies

If you're lucky enough to have a newborn, you can expect hordes of people to stop you in order to gawk at how adorable your offspring is. And, of course, since they are, you nod along appreciatively.

But, in some parts of the world, that exchange might be a little different.

In several countries across Eastern Europe and Asia, people believe that calling a baby "cute" might raise the ire and envy of evil spirits, prompting them to steal your baby. Therefore, people in these places will gleefully inform you how ugly your baby is, doing their part to protect it from malevolent forces.

Basically, these folks hold that evil spirits are vigilant when it comes to whatever a person holds dearest, and the presence of a cute baby provides a perfect opportunity to upset a blissful run. Evil spirits are pretty shallow, apparently.

This superstition ties in with a similar myth that calling a baby "cute" will lead to it being an ugly adult. Likewise, some hold that calling a baby well behaved will make it unruly when it gets older.

Once again, with this superstition we find a wide-spread belief that has no particular origin story and preys on a timeless concern: keeping children safe and happy. It's certainly a daunting task, and I imagine that for parents, the lack of control over a child's well-being provides fertile ground for magical thinking to grow.

I'm just glad infants don't start to make memories until later on in life. Recalling being called ugly over and over again is guaranteed to do some psychological damage, after all.

Fan Death

I need to sleep with a fan on. Even in the middle of a New England winter, you can count on a fan running right by my head. I love the white noise, and I need the room to be as cold as possible in order to get a good night's sleep.

If you, too, are from New England but can't imagine doing anything to increase the cold during those long, dark January nights, you might be sitting there, furiously shaking your head. But you may be surprised to know that there are many people in South Korea who would be even more appalled by my habit, regardless of season, and would consider my nocturnal fan use a death wish.

There's a decades-old superstition in South Korea that using an electric fan while your windows are closed can kill you—especially if it's by your head. The thinking is that the fan is filling the room with your own carbon dioxide and, with no way for oxygen to enter, you will eventually asphyxiate. Another faction believes that the fan could cause you to die from hypothermia.

An early account of this paranoia was published in a Korean newspaper in the 1920s. In it, the writer warned about the dangers of electric fans, claiming they caused maladies that range from nausea to death. Since then, several deaths where fans were coincidentally being used in enclosed spaces have been reported by South Korean news outlets, perpetuating the belief that a fan in an unventilated room is capable of dastardly acts.

The superstition's hold on the country has loosened considerably in recent years, but there are people who can't shake the feeling that something bad will happen if they have a fan on and don't open at least one window.

But evidence to the contrary is all around the world. Take me for example: my fan's running as I write this—door shut, windows shut, just me and my fan. So, either electric fans can't kill you, or this is the weirdest, most mundane afterlife I could ever imagine.

Flip the Baby

I love to sleep. And I don't mean to brag, but I'm great at it. So great I didn't even have to work at it—I always have been and, knock on wood (see page 42), always will be a champ at getting a good night's sleep. As it turns out, I may be able to thank this next superstition for my incredible talent.

According to one old wives' tale, flipping a baby upside down and briefly holding them that way will get them on a regular sleep cycle. To be perfectly clear, I don't mean parents desperate for some solid sack time should be involving their babies in any Cirque du Soleil–esque gymnastics. You can say a lot about the old wives, but you can't say they don't know how to care for a newborn.Instead, the myth holds that gently turning the baby in the air so that its feet are briefly pointed toward the sky is enough to change its, and your, sleep pattern.

In reality, a baby's ability to sleep on a regular schedule has nothing to do with whether they've been flipped or not (shocking, I know). Research has shown that babies do not develop their circadian rhythm—the release of hormones that indicate when it's time to turn in—until well after they're born.

So regardless of any baby flipping, you can probably count on losing at least a few weeks of solid sleep as your newborn develops.

I will say this, though: as I was doing research for this book, my own mother informed me about the existence of this one because she did it to me as a baby. Not only did I end up fine after my brief tumble, it set me on the path to join the greats of the sleep game. Thanks, Mom!

Knitting Outside Can Prolong Winter

Iceland is famous for many things: Björk, Wes Anderson–esque scenery, and geothermal power. But yarn is arguably the most accessible export from the island nation. Which is understandable: Iceland is known for extreme winter weather, meaning good sweaters composed of hearty yarn are not just a fashion statement, they're a necessity.

Because of the extreme conditions that prevail on the island, it makes sense that Icelanders both respect and fear the weather, a combination that is ripe for the formation of superstitions. One of the more interesting ones is connected to sweaters and holds that knitting these garments must be done strictly within the household during the winter months; otherwise, the harsh weather will be painfully prolonged.

First of all, I'm not sure who's eager to knit outdoors in the winter anywhere, let alone in Iceland. Knitting requires a fair amount of dexterity, and no matter how hardy you believe yourself to be, your fingers are bound to lose some of their nimbleness if you're just sitting outside in the middle of the winter. Has outdoor knitting in the winter ever been a recurring issue anywhere?

But I digress.

Unlike Punxsutawney Phil and his shadow (see page 25), these brazen knitters don't seem to add a specific amount of time onto winter. But I can only imagine that any added time is too much. There also does not seem to be a specific point of origin for this belief. Most likely some Icelander somewhere saw their neighbor knitting on their porch in what seemed to be late in the season, then suffered through a longer-than-usual extension of winter and connected the two events. I can't say I blame them.

In any case, keep those knitting needles indoors in the weeks before spring is due to arrive.

Safety Pins &
Red Underwear

There is perhaps no state where we are more vulnerable than having a baby. Between the birthing process, which can be a little embarrassing at best and deadly at worse, to the long-lasting effects of early-stage parenting, there are so many fraught things when it comes to child rearing. That said, it makes sense that there are superstitions about how you can have a smooth pregnancy and protect your child after giving birth.

There's a myth originally from Mexico and parts of Central America that a lunar eclipse is dangerous for babies in the womb, and therefore pregnant people should wear a safety pin fixed to the stomach of their shirt (near the bellybutton) as well as red underwear in order to protect their unborn child from evil spirits.

The red undergarment part of this belief seems to be tied to the Ancient Mayan belief that red symbolizes blood and the sun, a combination which signifies life. Metal, on the other hand, has been used as a means of protection across the globe throughout history, viewed as a gift from the divine that is also capable of warding off evil forces for centuries. In this light, a safety pin is just a convenient way to acquire this protection.

But what's so bad about an eclipse?

Before eclipse hunting became a thing in the modern world, this natural phenomenon was considered a sign of the apocalypse. Just imagine: you're in your home and all of a sudden, seemingly out of nowhere, the sky turns dark red and the sun and moon become one. In the absence of a scientific explanation, fears about the end of the world and evil spirits coming to take over easily took root during these events. Fray Bernardino de Sahagún, a fifteenth century Spanish writer and friar, described a truly frightening and disturbing scene in one Aztec community during an eclipse: "It was thus said: 'if the eclipse of the sun is complete it will be dark forever, the demons of darkness will come down. They will eat men!'"

While it's not clear why pregnant people and babies were most susceptible to the presumed negative effects of an eclipse, I reckon it has something to do with the tenuous and unpredictable nature of pregnancy and childbirth. Once again, here is an experience that—to this day—is shrouded in mystery, uncertainty, and even ignorance. So, in the face of the unexplainable, it makes sense that people would search for ways to protect the most vulnerable among them, even if it's just putting a safety pin on your shirt. Otherwise, it was believed that the child would suffer a range of afflictions from cleft lip to possession.

At this point, this superstition has become less of an actual belief, and more like a tradition, a practice that is passed down through the generations. But with all the uncertainty in the world right now, what's the harm in a little extra protection for your unborn child?

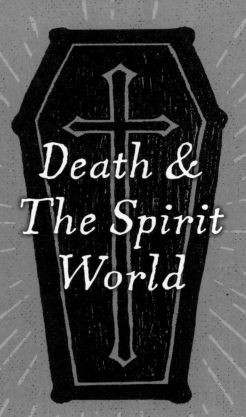

Death &
The Spirit
World

No Whistling Inside

One of my favorite scenes in Quentin Tarantino's *Kill Bill* is where Elle Driver, a member of the Deadly Viper Assassination Squad, is walking down a hospital corridor dressed in all white and whistling the chilling theme to the 1968 thriller *Twisted Nerve*. Like an angel of death, Elle makes a quick pitstop to change into an over-the-top nurse's uniform and carries a death-filled syringe into the room of The Bride, who's been in a 4-year coma after being ambushed by her fellow assassins. Elle intends to end The Bride's life once and for all, but she is ordered to stop just before she can inject the poison into her veins, leaving Elle and the rest of the Squad vulnerable to bloody revenge should The Bride miraculously wake up.

The scene is sleek, sinister, and plays right into a common superstition: whistling indoors is a serious harbinger of doom.

Some people believe that it's bad luck to whistle indoors, and each has its own belief in what bad thing will happen if you do. In parts of Eastern Europe, for example, people believe that whistling inside will throw you into financial ruin or even result in your house burning down. Some people believe it has to do with calling on evil spirits, like the superstition about whistling at night (see page 142), but for the most part, the reason and origin for this myth are a mystery.

Psychologically speaking, there's not much known about whistling, why we do it, and why some people simply can't stand it. Despite the assumption that people whistle when they're happy, most research has shown that whistling is more likely a regulating, self-soothing behavior rather than an expression of joy. Whistling has also historically been a form of human communication across the globe because the sound it produces has the ability to travel long distances.

Putting all this together, you might begin to understand why someone would feel uneasy about you whistling indoors, spiritual beliefs aside. It's close quarters, for starters. But, as you likely know, when someone around you feels uneasy, it's easier for other people to grow anxious, which could in turn lead to some unintentional disaster caused by anxiety and/or inattention. Maybe you're cooking, for example, hear your partner whistling in another room and, distracted by the unsettling tune, you absentmindedly put a dish cloth on the stovetop and it catches fire. Hey, it could happen!

In the absence of a clear origin story for this myth, I think that's a reasonable explanation. Besides, things didn't exactly turn out favorably for Elle Driver, either.

So the next time you feel the need to let loose and whistle that new earworm, step outside and entertain the smoking section. Better to be safe than sorry.

The Evil Eye

As someone of Moroccan descent, I am very aware of the threat the evil eye poses. My late grandmother was quite gifted at sensing when the evil eye had been cast upon a member of the family, and counteracted the curse with prayer. Her work was mysterious but surprisingly effective, as one particularly miraculous recovery from a case of food poisoning showed me. And as a kid, I was gifted a necklace with the classic blue-and-white evil eye pendant, which I still have to this day.

So, what exactly is the evil eye, then? Is it a curse or an object?

It happens to be both.

The evil eye is an overarching term for negative thoughts or looks tinged with envy, either for the life you live or the things you own. While each culture has its own take on who can cast the evil eye and how—sometimes, it is a power reserved for shamans; In other cultures, it is available to all, and can even be cast accidentally—the consequences are roughly the same across the board; many people believe the curse can cause real harm, from accidents to severe illness and death.

But the evil eye also refers to the actual talisman that you can wear as a necklace or bracelet, or hang in your home for protection against the evil eye itself. The earliest origins of the evil eye talisman and its protective properties can be traced back to ancient civilizations from Mesopotamia to Greece, where it was believed that the human eye could cast invisible rays of energy that were strong enough to kill. The eye-shaped talisman, meanwhile, was capable of counteracting this deadly power with its own potent rays. Most often, these talismans come in a beautiful, azure blue—a tradition that can be traced back to Turkish artisans roughly 3,000 years ago, who fashioned them as a tribute to Tengri, a god whose name was synonymous with "sky."

So, whether you wear an evil eye charm for protection, fashion, or both, rest assured that your accessory's ability to keep you safe is backed by centuries of faith and strength.

Ghost Month

On the seventh month of the lunar year, all hell breaks loose (literally) in various Asian countries. For these 30 days, folks remain on edge as they try to appease the spirits who have been granted a brief window to dwell among the living. Ghost Month, as it's called, is no joke. And if you're planning on heading over to Asia during it, you'll be wise to be well versed in the mythology surrounding it.

The origins of Ghost Month can be traced back to early Buddhist beliefs, which posited that there are hungry ghosts out there, spirits that are forced to suffer eternal starvation due to greed in their earthly lives. The 15th day of Ghost Month revolves around properly feeding these unfortunate souls so that they will proceed with other business and leave you alone for the rest of the year. In addition to elaborate meals and rituals, there may also be burlesque shows put on to entertain the spirits.

Much like Mexico's *Dìas de los Muertos*, and the original spirit of Halloween, Ghost Month is meant to be a time to remember and honor the dead, and for people to openly discuss and consider something that is typically taboo.

So, what are some of the things you shouldn't do during Ghost Month? As in Fight Club, one of the first rules of Ghost Month is that you can't talk about ghosts. Really. In fact, it's considered rude to call the spirits "ghosts." Instead, one should refer to them as "good brothers" or "good sisters." Holding big events like weddings, starting a new venture, or moving into a new home are also off-limits during the month. On a day-to-day basis, it's a good idea to avoid hanging lanterns or wind chimes around your house, and to avoid ever being in the dark. All of these things are said to attract good brothers and sisters (who may or may not be malevolent) to your home and away from the temples where they can rest.

By the end of the month, just as the portal between the living and the dead closes, it's customary for people to burn money as an offering to the spirits. Once the gates of the underworld are closed, it's right back to normal ... until next year.

Ghost Light

If you've ever been to an old theater, you know how beautiful they can be. Often, they possess intricate craftsmanship that you just never see in newer buildings. But they can also be creepy. Sometimes, when you're the only one in a theater, it's easy to feel like you're not completely alone. Don't worry too much though. The crew has installed something to protect you: the ghost light.

Ghost lights are those eerie lightbulbs that sit in the center of the stage, dimly illuminating the immediate surroundings even when the rest of the space is pitch black. Just about every theater around the world has one, because just about everyone involved with theater believes that without one, you're asking for trouble.

While there's no doubt that it's very practical to have this always-illuminated light in a theater, the main thrust behind this tradition is for it to serve as a sort of spiritual shield when a theater is empty, warding off mischievous spirits that could potentially gather and sabotage a production.

Ridiculous, you say? Well, as you may have heard (see page 149 and 151), the theater, due to the considerable anxieties it produces, is rife with superstitions and magical thinking. There are some believers in the ghost light that claim it isn't a matter of protecting the living from malevolent ghouls, but simply a kind gesture to the deceased who invariably inhabit the theater, lighting the space so they can go about their ghostly routines in peace and safety, and keep from accidentally bumping into the goings-on occurring in the material realm.

At the end of the day, though, whether one believes the ghost light is meant to keep spirits away or help them out, there is little doubt that they are there in the theater, and always a threat to upset the fragile balance of a production.

The Ouija Board Demon

Has the temperature in your room suddenly dropped? Are your windows shattering for seemingly no reason? Are you or your loved ones waking up with inexplicable scratches all over your body? If you answered "yes" to any of these questions, you may be being haunted by Zozo, the Ouija board demon.

Zozo is a mysterious and malicious demon that can only be summoned while using a Ouija board. So, he's pretty easy to avoid, but once he's made contact, he can make your life a living hell. Just ask Darren Evans from Oklahoma.

Evans is largely credited with bringing the legend of Zozo into the public eye after posting the story of his alleged encounters with the demon on a forum called "True Ghost Stories" in 2009. The post details initially innocuous and even pleasant interactions with what Evans thought was a friendly spirit or even the spirit of someone he had intended to contact. Ultimately, though, the interactions became more hostile, as Zozo revealed himself through clear threats to Evans, his ex-wife, and his then-infant daughter, who allegedly experienced several life-threatening incidents following a particularly intense interaction with the demon.

The post on the original forum has amassed hundreds of replies sharing similar stories and encounters with a spirit that either directly introduced itself as Zozo (well before they had even been aware of the name, they say) as well as the strange and downright evil things that have happened to them after making contact. There are also accounts of people being contacted not by Zozo, but by spirits with similarly repetitive names like Zaza or Mama, and then experiencing very similar phenomena to what people reported in the thread related to Evans' encounter. Many people believe that Zozo uses aliases so he can infiltrate the living world without raising suspicions.

Besides a potential reference to Zozo in an early nineteenth century French publication, and speculation around the demon being the influence for famous horror tales like *The Exorcist,* there is not much else known about this alleged Ouija board demon, where he comes from, or what he wants. It's very possible that Zozo is just an Internet legend meant to give you a fright. But if you're reading this and eager to give the ol' Ouija board a whirl, be sure to look up the rules before you get started. And, if you're worried you'll contact Zozo accidentally, just put the board back in the closet and walk away. You probably won't like anything you find.

Sin Eating & Funeral Biscuits

No, Sin Eaters are not the bad guys in a cut-rate Harry Potter knock-off. And, while the term makes for a great band name, that's also not what it is. Instead, Sin Eaters were everyday people, like you and me, who would symbolically consume the misdeeds of someone recently deceased in order to guarantee them an easy passage into the afterlife. Often, this thankless role was assigned to one person in the village who would be hired to attend local funerals and eat food, usually bread, that was served directly on or around the corpse, symbolically eating away the sins that this person carried in life.

Sin Eaters were fairly common across the United Kingdom and in other parts of Europe in the eighteenth and nineteenth centuries. The person who filled that role was often a pariah in the community because they willingly took on sins for money—as though they were the devil's mercenaries. That said, these brave and/or apathetic souls were called upon by families to ensure that their deceased loved ones gained swift entry into heaven, particularly when their death was sudden, since, theoretically, they hadn't had a chance to be absolved of their sins before passing.

Even though sin eating came from a desire to help the deceased into heaven, the various Christian churches were not thrilled by the practice and, in some cases, considered it heretical. It was never outright banned, but sin eating became taboo, with the church eventually linking it to the practice of magic. As such, the last known sin eater that practiced in the UK died in the early twentieth century, and there have not been any additional records of this practice since.

A somewhat related ritual practiced at the time put the responsibility of sin eating on all of the attendees at the funeral, in the form of "funeral biscuits" or "funeral cookies." These "treats" were individually wrapped with white paper and a black wax seal, and were served by the deceased's family as a way to both honor the departed and, in some cases, help them into the afterlife. This Victorian-era tradition made its way from Europe to North America, and there were several different cookie recipes that became popular depending on the location and economic status.

Both of these rituals have largely died out in modern society, where our stance toward death and dying has become so sanitized that these sorts of traditions seem really bizarre and macabre. Regardless, it is interesting to consider the role food and eating have played in mourning rituals across time and geography. We eat when we are grieving, but what does it mean? And who is it for?

Pele's Curse

Going to Hawaii is like being transported to another planet. Between the gorgeous beaches, the unique wildlife, and the active volcanoes dotted throughout the islands, you're bound to have your mind blown at least once a day during your stay. It's so memorable, you might even be tempted to find a piece of the island's natural beauty to take home with you as a souvenir. But it'd be wise to ignore that impulse and just stick to what's in the gift shop ... unless you want to feel the wrath of Pele.

Pele, the Hawaiian goddess of fire and volcanoes, is also considered both the creator and the protector of the islands. As such, native Hawaiians and locals have a tremendous amount of respect for the environment, as they consider the land—every single lava rock, grain of sand, and seashell—to be an extension of Pele herself. Therefore, taking a rock or shell back home with you is considered a transgression with cosmic consequences.

And Pele is not one to take this theft lightly.

Pele's Curse is the term people use to refer to the range of misfortunes that allegedly befall those who take pieces of the islands home with them. These misfortunes can range from minor inconveniences to life-threatening incidents, and are rumored to be unyielding so long as the stolen item is still in your possession. According to the legend, the only way to reverse the curse is to return the item to the islands. As such, Hawaiian post offices regularly receive packages from faraway lands containing these items and letters asking for Pele's forgiveness.

A quick search on sites like Reddit and YouTube will reveal countless stories of people who have allegedly experienced Pele's Curse firsthand. From car crashes and pink eye to severed limbs, the goddess's alleged victims are legion, and desperate to warn others against disturbing Pele's peace. However, there are just as many that allege the curse is made up and perpetuated by park rangers who do not want tourists

disturbing the environment, which is a reasonable explanation. And, as we all know, taking natural material from one place and bringing it to another risks introducing invasive species to your hometown and doing severe damage to the environment.

Additionally, there are some indigenous Hawaiians who consider the myth of Pele's Curse completely offensive and believe the curse has been used to exoticize an unlawful and disrespectful act for the sake of tantalizing tourists. I'm not Hawaiian myself, but I do tend to look down on these sorts of myths because they often only exist in the tourism industry, specifically when it comes to interacting with native cultures. It's unfortunate that the only way for the locals to earn respect is to give tourists a thrill—then they only care because something bad happened to them.

Anywho ... regardless of where you stand on Pele's Curse, I think the least you can do is be respectful of the locals and the environment. So, for everyone's sake, leave the lava rocks behind and stick to the souvenir T-shirts. Everyone will be a lot happier and safer that way.

No Whistling at Night

If you're walking down the street alone at night, one of the last things you want to hear is someone whistling. Even if it's your favorite song in the whole world, hearing that eerie, high-pitched, slightly off-tune whistle echo through the darkness is enough to give even the bravest among us chills. And with good reason—in many parts of the world, that whistler is allegedly attempting to summon something malevolent.

From East Asia to South America—which is about as widespread as any superstition I've found—people hold the belief that whistling at night summons evil spirits and/or Satan. There are, of course, some variations to this myth. In countries like China and Korea, people believe whistling will attract wandering spirits, who will end up following you home. Across parts of the Middle East and North Africa, people believe that whistling at night will attract the Devil himself. All in all, just about every culture that follows this myth believes that whistling at night is a way to attract unwanted and haunted guests.

As you might expect from a superstition that has worked its way into so many cultures, the origins of this myth are unclear. But it seems to have something to do with the long-held belief that the divide between this world and the spirit world is weakest in the middle of the night. As such, it makes sense that anything that could disrupt spirits or make them angry (i.e., loud, out-of-tune whistling in the middle of the night), would be deemed a spiritually unsafe thing to do, potentially putting you and your family at grave risk.

Either that, or someone really hated the sound of a whistle piercing the silence in the dead of night and came up with this story to make everyone cut it out.

Pagpag

I think we can all agree that funerals and wakes are utterly exhausting. Whether you're actively grieving the death of a loved one or trying to console those left behind, these services can take a lot out of you physically, emotionally, and financially. By the end, all you want to do is go home and lie down—not head out to a bar or restaurant.

But in the Philippines, a post-wake pitstop is a necessity if you want to keep death out of your own home.

The belief that you shouldn't go straight home after a service is called *pagpag*, and claims that the only way to prevent the dead from following you home is by stopping somewhere—anywhere—before you return home. A Tagalog word that literally translates to "shaking off dust or dirt," *pagpag* is quite literally the practice of shaking off death and bad energy that may have tried to hitch a ride back to your place after the funeral.

It's not clear where this particular superstition comes from, but it is still practiced by most Filipino families, both those living in the Philippines and across the diaspora. Fuzzy origins aside, the practice makes a lot of sense. Death and dying aren't topics you want to spend too much time thinking about for your own self-preservation. It's possible that by heading to another place before you go home, you're offering yourself a reprieve from the tragedy and a moment to let go of some of those thoughts before you return to your regularly scheduled life.

If you're curious about what could happen if you don't heed this superstition, there's a 2013 film called *Pagpag: Siyam na Buhay* that centers around a group of people who don't abide by the tradition and head straight home after a service. Spoiler alert: it's a bad time, at least for the living.

Hide Your Thumb

Seeing a hearse drive past you is pretty grim, and most people, regardless of where they're from, become uneasy at the prospect of this memento mori. But one country in particular takes this unease around hearses to a whole new level. One superstition from Japan states that, in order to avoid any bad luck associated with these distinctive vehicles, you should tuck your thumb into your fist when you see one about to pass you—unless you want your parents to die.

The word for "thumb" in Japanese roughly translates to "parent finger," which connects specifically to the idea that your parents will die if you don't hide your thumb. Otherwise, there do not seem to be specific theories as to how this superstition came to be. So, besides a generous interpretation of the word, there's not much else to go on.

However, there does seem to be a connection between fingers and malevolent spirits. In some cultures, the thumb is referred to as the "devil's finger," since its dexterity facilitates so much of man's wickedness. And, as explained in the entry regarding Japan's strict avoidance of cutting your fingernails at night on page 111, our digits seem to provide bridges to the spirit world. Perhaps this superstition melds these finger-related anxieties with the concept of the "parent finger," and, sensing that this means one's parents are potentially in danger, does it's best to deny the spiritual world all access to the thumb.

Some people will also hide their thumbs as they walk past graveyards to avoid passing along a similar fate to their parents. It's a bit odd, but it certainly sounds a lot healthier than trying to hold your breath along the entire length of a cemetery (see page 147).

Wearing Black at a Funeral

How many times have you innocuously worn all black (because, let's face it, you look incredible in it) and been asked, "Who died?" For me, it's happened at least a couple dozen times.

The reason most people in the West readily associate wearing black with mourning comes from a combination of ancient ritual and superstition. Ancient Romans would wear black togas as a sign that they were in mourning. This ritual then spread throughout the Roman Empire and remained the prevailing tradition once the empire fell and Europe took shape. By the Victorian era, this expression of mourning became entwined with a supernatural belief that spirits would attend funeral services to help usher the recently deceased into the afterlife. Wearing black as a living person was a way to disguise yourself from being influenced and/or accidently escorted by the spirits to the Great Beyond.

Wearing black is still synonymous with funerals in most parts of the world, mostly out of habit and respect for tradition. But it's far from universal. In China, it's common to see people dressed in white as they mourn, though they might wear red or pink if the deceased was over the age of 80, as those colors signify happiness, and celebrate a long life that was well lived. We also see white used in Indigenous Australian mourning, as widows would wear white plaster caps called kopis anywhere between a week to six months after the loss of their partner.

Next time someone teases you for wearing all black, just whip out some of these funeral facts and I bet they'll get off your case. I can't say that it will make you seem any less morbid for knowing so much about funerals, but it will probably keep you from getting asked the same thing over and over again, allowing you to live out your life as the black-wearing fashionista you are!

Holding Your Breath Past the Cemetery

Cemeteries are a daily reminder of our own mortality. And, whether you believe in ghosts or not, you have to admit there is something spooky about being in or near a cemetery—a quality about the air there that seems different and otherworldly—which is why folk wisdom instructs you to hold your breath when you go past one. If you don't, you could make the dead jealous or worse: you could end up inhaling the spirit of someone who recently passed away.

If you've read the other entries up to this point, you've probably noticed this strange link between breathing and spirits. The connection seems to link back to the Old Testament, where God brought Adam to life by breathing into him. It's perhaps no coincidence then that in Hebrew, the word for breath and spirit are the same (ruach).

But you don't need to be religious or even spiritual to feel the connection between breath, life, and the metaphysical. When we stop breathing, all the things that make up a soul—our personality, our thoughts, our feelings, those ineffable things that make us human—they go away, too. Without breath, our souls are unknowable because they do not exist. At least, not in a way that we can interact with. In a more secular sense, we can generally connect to our thoughts and feelings better when we take a moment to focus on our breathing, grounding us in time and place, and to our general sense of being.

So, it makes some sense that a restless, recently deceased soul would want to and be able to attach itself to a living person's breath. Though you certainly have to wonder what kind of spirit would be willing to take another soul's place just for a little more time on Earth. Envy isn't only for the living, apparently.

Red Ink Death Threat

Fans of the Japanese anime/manga *Death Note* might be surprised to learn that in South Korea, you don't even need a magic book from a shinigami to play God.

There's a superstition that writing someone's name in red ink is as good as handing down a death sentence. Historically, a person's name was only ever written in red ink on official death certificates—no ifs, ands, or buts. As such, even if you are completely ignorant of the malicious history and the person behind the name is the picture of health, writing someone's name in red ink is viewed with grave seriousness, akin to trying to kill the person.

As you might have guessed, the nearly universal association between red and violence has also helped this superstition take off. While you might

think black to be more fitting for
a death decree, the aggres-
sion and gore associated
with red gives it a dimen-
sion that black ink, despite
its connection to the macabre, just doesn't convey.

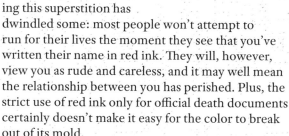

Over the years, the fear
and seriousness surround-
ing this superstition has
dwindled some: most people won't attempt to
run for their lives the moment they see that you've
written their name in red ink. They will, however,
view you as rude and careless, and it may well mean
the relationship between you has perished. Plus, the
strict use of red ink only for official death documents
certainly doesn't make it easy for the color to break
out of its mold.

Future teachers in Korea, take note: leave the red
pens behind. You wouldn't want to mark your students for an early demise. Or maybe you would, in
which case I'd suggest finding a new profession.

Bad Luck to Say Good Luck

There are certain rules you're expected to follow
when you go to the theater. Most of them are meant
to keep you from distracting the actors, like no
talking during the performance, turning your phone
off, and no flash photography.

But there's one rule that stands above all: never, ever wish a performer good luck before a show. Indeed, the admonition was immortalized in Mel Brooks's *The Producers*: "it's bad luck to say good luck on opening night / If you do, I'll tell you / It is certain by the curtain / You are through."

Outside the theater, "good luck" is an innocuous phrase. It's something you might off-handedly say to your spouse as they head to the mall on Black Friday, or when your co-worker is summoned to a meeting with the boss. So, what's the big deal about saying it at a performance?

For starters, theater culture is rife with superstitions and myths, and many theater makers strongly believe that ghosts and spirits haunt every stage. One theory behind the superstition is that some of these alleged spirits will latch onto any good luck wishes and then make the exact opposite happen, often in the form of bad reviews or even bodily harm. This superstition is a lot like one from Eastern Europe where people will call babies ugly in order to fend off malevolent spirits (see page 120).

But I, as a former theater kid, think there could be something else going on. As if getting in front of an audience isn't hard enough, I think anything you say or do that could even remotely throw you off your game before the show is going to have an impact on your performance. It's possible that this caustic mix of pre-show anxiety, the burden of entertaining paying audience members, and being wished "good luck" can cause you to focus so intensely on any one thing that goes wrong that the "good luck" superstition becomes a bit of a self-fulfilling prophecy. I believe this because I guarantee just about everyone who performs has a story or knows someone who had the worst performance of their life after someone wished them "good luck."

So, what can you say instead? If you've spent any time in or around a theater, you've probably heard someone say "break a leg." Despite how violent and unpleasant it sounds, no legs will be broken at the command. The phrase allegedly comes from Ancient Greece, where enthused audience members would stomp loudly as a form of applause. The story goes that if the show was exceptionally good, the audience would stomp their feet so hard that they'd break their legs.

Another popular phrase is "*merde*," the French word for "shit." Gross, right? Yes, but you'll probably make a performer's day if you say this to them before they head on stage.

The Curse of the Scottish Play

While we're at the theater, you'll also want to avoid saying the title of a certain Shakespearean play. You know, the bloody one. Based in Scotland. With the witches. Must I go on?

Yes, many people believe that saying "Macbeth" in a theater will bring that person, and potentially those around them, extremely bad luck.

Macbeth is one of William Shakespeare's best-known tragedies, and for centuries it has served as ripe source material for academics and others to explore madness, ambition, and power dynamics.

For anyone who needs a refresher, the play is about a nobleman (Macbeth) who receives a surprising prophecy from three witches that he will become king. Eager to speed up the process, he and his wife decide to kill the current king while he is staying as a guest at their home. However, once Macbeth does the deed and is crowned king, he is overcome by guilt and paranoia. Macbeth's outbursts and increasingly unhinged behavior draw suspicion from those around him, and he is eventually ambushed by a coup, and he himself is ultimately killed, allowing the rightful heir to assume the throne.

It's not exactly a light-hearted romp. But it certainly is a thrill to watch and/or read.

The belief that saying "Macbeth" in the theater is bad luck dates back to the very first production of the play around 1606.

Allegedly, the actor that was supposed to play Lady Macbeth died suddenly, forcing Shakespeare himself to fill the role at the last minute (all roles in that era were played by men, so it's not as bizarre a casting choice as it seems today). Since then, there have been several high-profile incidents during productions of the play, including fake weapons being replaced with real weapons, set pieces falling, fights among cast members, accidents, and several other deaths before, during, and after performances of the play.

There are two main theories propelling this myth, both of which are themselves rooted in witchcraft. The first is that proper witches in England were upset by how Shakespeare depicted their community, so they cursed the play for eternity. The other theory is that the play was accidentally cursed by Shakespeare himself because he used real spells for the witches' dialogue.

So, if you're in a theater, try to remember not to say the actual name of the play; "the Scottish play" or "the Bard's play" are both much safer alternatives. If the name does accidentally slip out, all you have to do is leave the theater, spin around three times, spit over your left shoulder, and yell out a swear or a line from the play.

That should save you from the curse, but I can't say you'll be safe from fervent theater people in your proximity.

Watch What You Eat

Don't Burst Your Bubbles

The way your coffee or tea settles in your cup can have major implications on the rest of your day, at least according to customs in parts of Europe and the United Kingdom. Like the soothsaying abilities of coffee grounds and tea leaves, the bubbles that form on the surface of your morning beverage are powerful oracles, capable of predicting everything from love and financial outcomes to the weather.

Meaning in the bubbles has everything to do with their size and position in the cup, and the meaning you derive from these details can also depend on where you're from. For instance, people in Finland believe that if the bubbles move toward you, it means you'll be getting an influx of unexpected money soon. If they move away, you're destined to lose a hefty sum. People across the UK have a similar belief, but with the caveat that the number of bubbles that form in your coffee or tea make all the difference, determining the size of the gain or loss.

As for the weather, if the bubbles form in the center of the cup, it means it will be a sunny day. If they form on the edges of the cup, you can expect rain. While believers in these bubbly meteorologists say that their formation is influenced by atmospheric pressure, there's no scientific evidence that this is accurate. Additionally, atmospheric pressure is not a solid predictor of what kind of weather is on its way, which makes the theory even less solid.

Furthermore, it's unclear where the belief that coffee or tea bubbles determine your financial prospects or the day's weather began. But, considering that most people around the world start their days off with a cup of coffee or tea, and many different cultures use coffee grounds or tea leaves as a means of divination, it makes sense that we would turn to our morning beverages to enlighten us in any way possible—they already do such a wonderful job of getting us ready for the day, regardless of their magical properties!

The Right Way to Serve Bread

The French take bread very seriously, and that passion for the perfect loaf definitely pays off. If you've ever had the fortune of buying a freshly baked baguette from a Parisian bakery and eating it as you walk around the city, you'll know exactly what I mean.

This intensity about good bread also comes with a host of superstitions, including one that a loaf must always be served right side up. Otherwise, everyone present will be in for some serious bad luck.

This myth comes to us from the Middle Ages when bakers, instructed by authorities to feed the executioners, would turn one of the loaves upside down to signal to others that it belonged to the executioner. As you can imagine, executioners weren't exactly welcomed with open arms in most parts of society. It was said that the baker's hatred and distaste for these gruesome public employees seeped into the baguette, making it taste far worse than his regular creations. Even so, bakers would often intentionally put aside the worst baguettes in the batch for executioners, since they never paid for their bread anyway.

Add all these factors up—the general hatred of executioners, associations with death, and bakers' nightmares about serving bad bread—and it makes sense that the sight of an upside-down loaf would cause people to freak out. At best, an upside-down loaf means that the bread's probably not that good. At worst, it could mean an encounter with death itself is around the corner. I mean, can you imagine what an interaction with a hangry French executioner would be like after you swiped his bread?

Nonetheless, no loaf of bread is beyond saving, even if it is upside down. Apparently, the way to reverse any potential harm is to take a knife and draw a cross on the flat side of the bread. There are also some people who just turn the loaf over when they see upside-down bread in a bakery, so that the person who goes to take it will not be cursed.

So, if you ever find yourself in a French bakery and all you can find is upside-down bread, no need to despair. Just take out your knife and exorcise that loaf! It'll still probably be one of the best things you've ever eaten.

Spilled Salt

Between the health consequences and the superstitions, it might be best to keep a healthy distance from salt. The myth that spilling salt is bad luck seems to be one of those superstitions that everybody knows, but which has no specific origin. However, examining the role of salt in historical and cultural contexts, we can get a pretty good idea of how it came to be.

First, salt has a long association with good fortune, and in Christianity it is closely associated with God. That's why when you do spill salt, you need to throw some over your left shoulder in order to "blind the devil." As far as protective superstitions go, salt's closeness to God and associations with purity mean it has been used to create barriers against evil spirits around the world for centuries. In Japan, it's customary for sumo wrestlers to throw salt in the ring before a match in order to purify the space. Salt has also been used to protect against the evil eye and cleanse homes that have been affected by it.

Beyond its symbolic weight, salt was invaluable for much of history because of its ability to prevent food rot and decay. As a result, it's possible that people started to exaggerate this ability and began to believe that salt prevented death and loss in all instances, hence its use as a good luck token for travel and new beginnings. The combination of its practical and spiritual protective properties made salt extremely valuable, so getting your hands on some was considered a sign of good fortune. In fact, the word "salary" comes from the Roman practice of paying soldiers in salt.

Nowadays, salt is ubiquitous enough that we're encouraged to avoid it as often as possible, and it certainly wouldn't be an acceptable form of payment for services rendered. But the abundance of this mineral still hasn't helped us feel any less horrified when someone spills it. So, for your own health and good fortune, be sure to pass the salt mindfully.

Spill the Tea

As an adult, my go-to beverage tends to be a cup of coffee. Still, there's something special and vaguely magical about tea, something peaceful that lends itself to feelings of gratitude and peace. In all seriousness, I believe that tea drinking has contributed to the person I am, and the person I'm becoming.

It's probably a sentiment many people across the globe can relate to because, in addition to the incredible array of flavors they can release when steeped in boiled water, tea leaves have been considered a useful tool in divination and other supernatural practices for centuries. Tea leaf reading, for instance, is a form of divination in which the leaves left in a person's cup after they've drunk their tea can provide insight into that person's life, whether it be love or work.

Some people believe that you don't even have to drink tea in order to reap the benefit of its magical powers. An old superstition in England holds that spilling tea leaves provides protection from evil spirits. As such, people would put tea leaves in front of their doors or around their home and in a departure from the numerous superstitions that caution against spilling food in your home, some also believe that spilling tea leaves inside would bring you good luck and extra protection. It had to be an accidental spill, though.

Otherwise, you were just making a mess.

It appears that using tea leaves as a form of protection was most common in nineteenth century
England, but the trail doesn't extend any further
than that, so it's unclear what the precise origin
of this superstition is. However, when we add the
history of tea leaves being linked to magic and divination to the extensive history of plants and herbs
being used for protection in just about every corner
of the globe, it seems likely that those people who
made the practice notable during the nineteenth
century simply turned to the most accessible and
disposable group of herbs they could find—it is
England, after all—and used it as a homegrown rem-
edy against negative energy.

Makes sense. Still, I like to imagine that the tea is
providing the bad energy itself the same boost of
energy and joy it provides us. After all, how do you
know a demon can't be feel chuffed after a piping
hot mug of Earl Grey?

No Singing at the Table

Sure, you sing like an angel. Even still, nobody wants
to hear you belt out "I Will Always Love You" at the
dinner table. For starters, you could choke. Plus,
some people already have a hard enough time deal-
ing with the sounds of people chewing (a malady
known as misophonia)—being forced to hear you
try and hit that high C in the chorus might just push
them over the edge.

In the Netherlands, there's another pitfall of singing at the dinner table: you just might be performing for the devil himself.

This Dutch superstition posits that singing at the dinner table means you're praising the devil for your meal, which, obviously, could leave you vulnerable to other evil spirits. Beyond the serious mental gymnastics backing this assertion, there isn't a lot of information about the origins or background of this belief, which leads me to conclude that this is one of those superstitions meant to scare people away from doing something that would irk most people—a common origin for superstitions.

Just like when your parents tell you not to roll your eyes or "they'll get stuck up there" (I heard that one a lot growing up), or how some families use the Elf on the Shelf to make sure their kids behave during the holiday season, superstitions often stem from a desire to deter unwanted behavior. Yes, it's manipulative. And we could certainly debate the ethics of scaring people into obedience. But I think the biggest takeaway from this, and other etiquette-related superstitions is just how powerful a story can be—how quickly it spreads, and how firmly it sticks in a group's consciousness.

While I can't guarantee that not singing at the dinner table will keep the devil away, I can say with some confidence that doing so will make everyone you're breaking bread with a lot happier. Save the concert for the ride back home.

Deadly Chopsticks

Chopsticks are the eating utensil of choice throughout many parts of Asia. If you're not accustomed to using them, it can be pretty difficult to use them correctly. And, as if maneuvering them wasn't hard enough, there's also plenty of etiquette to keep in mind while you're doing your best to bring food from the bowl to your mouth, such as not rubbing the chopsticks together, and not stabbing a piece of food with a single chopstick, among many others.

But there's one rule that you should never, ever do: don't stick your chopsticks upright in your food.

In addition to being considered very rude and simply incorrect, bowls of rice with chopsticks sticking upright are exclusively used as offerings at altars for the dead. Considered a last meal of sorts, the deceased person's loved ones present the food as a way of showing the spirit, which Buddhists believe remains conscious on Earth for some time before heading into the afterlife, that they are still loved.

In this context, the presentation is heartwarming. But elsewhere, it becomes troubling, as the sight of chopsticks stuck vertically into food at a restaurant or a person's home can potentially trigger upsetting memories of past funerals or of death itself, which, obviously, most people don't want to think about at dinner.

In addition to not sticking your chopsticks vertically into your food, it's also considered bad luck (and rude) to pass food from one pair of chopsticks to another, as this also resembles a funeral ritual. After a body is cremated, family members often pick through the ashes with pairs of chopsticks to remove the fragments of bone that are left. From there, each piece is passed around to each person via chopsticks, and then placed in an urn. So, if you must share food with someone at your table, make sure you have a separate plate available so you can place it down and pass it over, rather than handing it to them straight from your chopsticks.

Don't Drop That Tortilla

There's nothing quite like homemade tortilla. Once you try it, nothing else will do. Part of it is the pleasant combination of chewiness and pillowy texture. And another part is that the tortilla is one of those foods that is so guileless you can feel every bit of effort and consideration that went into making it. Because of this, every bite feels sacred. And, should something happen to it, it sort of feels like you've committed some grave violation.

People in Mexico are nodding along with this last bit: not just because the tortilla is an everyday staple in the country, but also because of a superstition

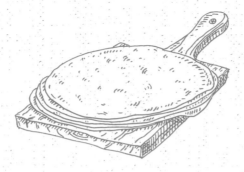

that if you drop a tortilla, you'll soon be visited by unwanted guests.

Some people believe that these "unwanted guests" are specifically your in-laws. But, of course, that cruel fate is only possible if you're married, and if you also happen to dislike your in-laws. Other iterations of this myth simply say that the visitors will come in the form of anyone you don't want to see, making an already brutal, tortilla-less day into an exceptionally crummy day.

I think this myth really is just a nod to the idea that one unfortunate thing caused by carelessness will beget more unfortunate things in the future. It's a gentle reminder to stay on the ball, and not let the products of your time and attention fall by the wayside. Should you violate this, and signal to the tortilla gods that your time is not all that valuable, you can kiss your dinner and any free time goodbye, because Karen is dropping by with a slideshow featuring all 4,000 pictures of her life-changing trip to the Grand Canyon. My condolences.

Sweet Dreams

Meeting the person of your dreams is a piece of [wedding] cake [under your pillow]!

There are many traditions associated with wedding cake: the newlywed couple must be the first to cut and eat the cake; couples should keep a piece of their cake and eat it on their first anniversary. This one, however, which is geared toward single people looking to settle down, is by far the messiest. According to this superstition, sleeping with a piece of wedding cake under your pillow will make you dream about the person you'll end up marrying.

This myth was most popular around the seventeenth century, when wedding cakes had no fluffy frosting and mousse and were a lot sturdier—similar to the much-maligned fruit cakes that appear around the holidays. In those days, pieces of wedding cake were often given out as favors rather than eaten at the reception, and people who were single were encouraged to slip it under their pillow for a night—a hybrid of the tooth fairy and catching the bride's bouquet.

It's not totally clear why wedding cake was the object that could provide a vision of your future beau. Maybe it was because cake was the one piece of the wedding people took home with them, so it was believed some properties of love and partnership became embedded in it. Maybe it's far more literal than that, and the slice of cake would promote "sweet dreams."

Whatever the reasoning, you probably won't see a bunch of single people today heading home with a slice of cake that they intend to sleep with, even though the wedding cake is still a major part of modern wedding celebrations. On the other hand, considering the trials and tribulations of modern dating, what's a little frosting all over your sheets if it means knowing who you'll marry?

Wish Upon a Bone

Bones. We can't live without them. And for millennia, bones have held a sacred place in the customs and rituals of civilizations across the world. While they are perhaps most often associated with death and/or danger, there are actually plenty of examples where bones serve as a symbol of life and creation. The Bible describes how God created Eve from a piece of Adam's rib, suggesting, of course, the object's tremendous power. We can also see bones used in divination rituals across Africa because of their ability to provide structure in the otherwise random and chaotic universe.

If we continue to follow that train of thought, we might consider all bones as possessing a sacred link to the divine, or at least as objects that ground us within something greater than ourselves. It should come as no surprise, then, that there are more than just a couple bone-related myths and superstitions around the world. Perhaps one of the best known in North America is the tradition of wishing on a wishbone. If you're someone who celebrates Thanksgiving in the United States, you've probably done this a handful of times. It involves two people holding opposite ends of the furcula—the V-shaped bone found between a turkey's neck and breast plate—and pulling until it breaks. The person who breaks off the larger side of the bone will have their wish granted.

The wishbone game has been a staple of Thanksgiving celebrations for centuries, but the interest in this particular bone goes all the way back to the Etruscans, an ancient Italian civilization that predated the Romans. In Etruscan society, it was common to remove the furcula from a recently slaughtered chicken and lay it out in the sun to dry. Anyone walking by who touched the bone was able to make a wish, hence the name "wishbone."

So next time you square off with your wishbone rival and start tugging away for the triumphant end of the bone, just know you're practicing an ancient ritual with spiritual roots that transcend any one time or place. Pretty cool, if you ask me.

Apples, Mirrors
& Marriage

If sleeping on a piece of wedding cake isn't quite your thing (see page 166), or you don't have any weddings to attend any time soon, there may be another way for you to envisage the person you'll marry. All you need is an apple, a mirror, a candle, a comb (sometimes), a knife, and an alarm loud enough to wake you up before midnight.

There are several apple-and-mirror rituals from around the world that are said to show you visions of your future lover. In parts of Asia, for instance, there's a belief that if you sit in front of a mirror at midnight with a lit candle and peel the skin off an apple in one strip, the image of your future lover will appear in the mirror. Though may I suggest that these visions are a result of the blood loss caused by trying to meticulously peel an apple in the dark?

There are several similar superstitions that come from the British Isles and North America, and were all tradi- tionally practiced on Halloween. One claims that if you eat an apple in front of a mirror while also combing your hair at midnight on All Hallows' Eve, you'll see your future husband or wife. Another one insists that if you peel an apple's skin off with a knife and then throw the peel over your left shoulder, the shape it lands in will be the first letter of your future spouse's name.

I could keep going. Seriously, there are many more. But I think you get the drift: apples, mirrors, midnight, soulmates. Any musicians out there, feel free to use it as the name of your first album.

Apples may seem like a random choice to some, but the fruit actually has an extensive history of being used to flesh out the shape of a person's life. For example, another superstition claims that if you cut an apple in half and count the seeds, you'll know how many children you're going to have. And, when you consider the apple's pivotal role in one of humanity's most famous myths—Adam and Eve's expulsion from the Garden of Eden—it makes sense that people would imbue this fruit with supernatural powers.

Apples are a symbol of knowledge, fertility, and sexuality. And when it comes to knowing who you'll spend the rest of your life with, whether you're taking your new fling out for a day of apple picking or sitting in a darkened room peeling an apple in front of a mirror at midnight, no other fruit will do.

Clouds in My Coffee

Just like getting pooped on by a bird (see page 37), accidentally spilling coffee can really ruin your day. Maybe it was still piping hot and you burned yourself. Maybe you stained your best shirt just before heading into a meeting with your boss. Or maybe you just really needed the caffeine.

But, as with bird poop, spilled coffee is considered an auspicious sign in some parts of the world. In some countries surrounding the Mediterranean and in the Middle East, especially in Egypt and Greece, your spilled cup of joe is generally a sign that good luck is coming your way. In Greece, the superstition holds that if you accidentally spill your drink, you're a hair away from falling into a fortune. You might also hear the people around you yell "*Gouri, gouri!*" the Greek term for "good luck," just to really drive home the point that you're on the road to riches.

While most other parts of the world just consider spilled coffee as you'd anticipate—a nuisance—there are some nuances that could change your fortune.

One superstition holds that if a woman happens to spill coffee, that means her lover is thinking about her. I personally wouldn't consider that "good luck" per se, but it's a nice sentiment. On the flip side, if you happen to drop a full cup of coffee, beware: you've not only made a terrific mess and probably destroyed your favorite mug, you've also cursed yourself with bad luck.

So, if you're a bit clumsy in the morning before that caffeine starts coursing through your veins, consider moving to a country where your inevitable mishap is seen as a positive.

Welcome Home, Here's Your Egg

A person arriving back home after a stint in the hospital has a lot on their to-do list: schedule follow-up appointments, pick up prescriptions from the pharmacy, update loved ones on their status. In Uganda, a person returning home from the hospital has one more thing they must do before settling back into their regular life: crush an egg under their foot.

This superstition claims that stepping on an egg will ensure that neither you nor any member of your family will ever again face the affliction that sent you to the hospital. Interestingly, former prisoners in the country also do this practice once they've served their time, in order to avoid being sent back to the slammer.

It's hard to determine exactly where this belief and practice comes from and how (or when) it started. However, as in most parts of the world, eggs are a powerful symbol in Ugandan culture. While eggs are, as you'd imagine, a symbol of fertility, they are also frequently associated with hope and renewal. Much like the UK sailors and civilians who've developed the habit of crushing eggshells to avoid a mishap at sea (see page 181), the Ugandan people who perform this welcome home ritual are ultimately seeking safe passage into the next chapter of their life. When we combine these associations, the act of stepping on an egg is essentially breaking open a new life for yourself—one that is ideally better, healthier, safer, and thus more joyous.

Minty Flesh

What do Hannibal Lecter and chewing gum at night have in common?

Yes, cannibalism is the correct answer.

There's a belief in Turkey that chewing gum at night is unlucky because it turns that piece of minty refreshment into something far less appetizing: human flesh. And if you're wondering how exactly chewing a piece of gum when it's dark out is even remotely like Dr. Lecter's penchant for the finer cuts of human meat, get in line. The origins of this superstition have been elusive to say the least, as are any details. For instance, does your piece of gum turn into flesh if you began chewing it in the daylight? Or is it just gum unwrapped in the evening that becomes flesh?

Also, unless you, too, enjoy having an old friend for dinner, I imagine that the moment a piece of Juicy Fruit turned to rotting flesh, you'd spit it out immediately, right?

Right??

In all seriousness, though, avoiding chewing gum at night follows a suite of allegedly unlucky activities the superstitious among us try to avoid once the sun sets, like clipping nails (see page 111) and sweeping the house (see page 117). In many cultures, night is when the barrier between the living world and the supernatural world is the thinnest, and it is also the time when most of the nefarious goings-on in the human world take place.

Apart from the spiritual considerations, there is a somewhat practical side to this myth. The point might be that there is a time and a place for everything, and the transformation of gum into flesh could just be the extreme version of otherwise sound advice.

That said, I think I'll be sticking to mints from now on. And only during the day, just to be extra safe.

Apologies to any of my future suitors ahead of time.

No Bananas on Board

Maybe it's the salt water. Maybe it's spending months out at sea with the same dozen faces. Whatever it is, there are plenty of myths that sailors have come to believe with their whole sea-faring hearts. One of those superstitions: it's bad luck to have bananas aboard a ship during a voyage.

This superstition can be traced back to the eighteenth century, just as the banana trade began to ramp up. One theory suggests that the myth gained momentum after multiple shipwrecks left nothing but bananas floating on the surface, leaving some sailors to conclude that the bananas had been the culprit of the wreck.

Some other theories are a little more grounded in reason. For one, because bananas spoil rather quickly, ships carrying the fruit had to move quickly to make sure they reached their destination before the bananas rotted. As a result, any fishermen aboard the ship were unable to properly execute their job. Bananas also release natural gases as they ripen, and some sailors believed that the gas could become deadly if the bananas were left on board for too long. While bananas do give off ethylene gas, which could be toxic in very high doses within tight quarters, the idea that they could knock out an entire ship is far-fetched. Still, others believed that poisonous spiders would hitch a ride on bananas and then wreak havoc once aboard.

Between the impracticalities inherent in transporting bananas to fears over the deadly threat they posed to everyone on board the ship, many sailors ended up banning the banana outright. Even today, there are sailors and recreational fishermen that refuse to allow bananas or banana-themed items on their boat over fears that they'll bring bad juju.

So, if you're planning to join a fishing charter this weekend, bring your Coppertone sunscreen rather than your Banana Boat, just to play it safe. And make sure to wipe Gwen Stefani's "Hollaback Girl" from your fishing trip playlist.

Nimbu Mirchi

When you're walking around India, it's not uncommon to see strings with a lemon and green chiles hanging from peoples' doorways. You might think it's for aesthetic purposes, or an inventive means of storage. But while I'm sure the vibrant blend of colors is plenty pretty, what you're seeing goes far beyond decoration. It's a talisman against disaster, dark magic, and the evil eye (see page 131).

People in India have been hanging a lemon and seven chilies—referred to as *nimbu mirchi*— outside

homes and businesses for centuries to ward off any bad luck headed their way, specifically from Alakshmi, the goddess of bad luck and misfortune. The myth surrounding the tradition relates that the menacing goddess and her benevolent sister, Lakshmi, once asked a merchant what makes each of them beautiful. The merchant, eager to get Lakshmi to stay and Alakshmi to leave, responded that Lakshmi looks beautiful as she comes inside from outside, while Alakshmi looks beautiful as she goes outside from inside. Well played, sir.

Furthermore, legend says that Alakshmi likes to snack on sour and spicy things. So, by hanging lemon and green chiles outside of the home, she can grab a snack while "looking her best," and, most importantly, keep out of homes and shops and move on without deciding to curse them with the evil eye.

Interestingly, lemons and chiles have historically offered more than just supernatural protection. Both foods were used as a sort of natural pesticide before the industrial stuff had been invented. As such, this talisman served this dual purpose of cleansing the area of bad energy and of pests.

Today, in addition to it hanging outside of homes and shops, you might even see *nimbu mirchi* dangling from the rearview mirror inside someone's car. And, for those who aren't keen on leaving produce hanging around, plastic or metal versions of the talisman are available. Just be aware: while they seem to do all right against Alakshmi, these artificial offerings make for terrible pesticides.

Stir with a Knife, Stir Up Strife

There are a surprising number of superstitions around the world involving knives. Maybe it's because of the dichotomy they present. On one hand, knives can be used to create, bringing people closer in ways both direct and indirect. But on the other hand, knives can be used to commit heinous acts; they can maim, kill, and cause irrevocable harm. They can even sever relationships (see page 57). Maybe that's why in the United Kingdom, it's considered bad luck to stir anything—tea, coffee, or a cocktail—with a knife.

This is one of those superstitions that everyone knows, but no one has any idea where it came from. Furthermore, the superstition has now taken hold in many different regions, so it's not clear if the belief comes from the UK specifically. But we do have the UK to thank for the simple little rhyme that will help us all remember: "stir with a knife, stir up strife."

The "strife" in question has not been defined. But considering it's the UK, perhaps it could be something like a particularly volatile argument over the proper way to prepare a scone: cream before jam, or jam before cream? For my own safety and well-being, I'll keep my two cents on the question to myself and move on.

I do think that there is some element of truth to the idea that seeing such a symbolically loaded utensil being used out of context can be unsettling. As we've seen with whistling at night (see page 142), the insertion of something seemingly harmless where it doesn't belong can disturb people enough that a powerful superstition forms around the prevention of it. I also think there's a practical element to this belief meant to keep people from having a bunch of wet knives hanging about. Imagine trying to slice some bread with a knife that someone had just used to stir their tea? Horrifying.

Also, where's your other cutlery? If you have a drawer full of forks, spoons, and knives, and you went for the latter to stir your Manhattan, I have questions.

El Ultimo

Sometimes we say things we don't mean. Other times, we say things we do mean but didn't want to say out loud. And then there are times when words leave plenty of room for interpretation—too much room, as in the case of the *el ultimo* myth.

El ultimo—"the final" in Spanish—is a Cuban superstition that appears most frequently in bars and clubs, instructing one to never announce that a drink is your last, because this declaration tempts fate and could, therefore, make this particular serve your last drink ever.

While I don't know enough Spanish to analyze the nuances of this phrase, it's clear that saying "this is my last drink" could acquire an ominous tinge in any language. Generally, I think it's safe to assume that when someone announces they're having their last drink, they almost certainly mean they're having their last drink of the night. But sometimes, the mind can't help but try and amplify the simplest things, transforming them into literally awesome and fearsome pronouncements. And, of course, the deep-rooted desire to avoid hubris makes us eager to search for ways to prevent it.

I appreciate the deep respect for the weight of words that his superstition shows. I also tip my hat to whomever was brilliant enough to combine the ambiguity of language and fears of death with a desire to keep the party going for as long as possible. After all, it's hard to leave a party if you can't tell your friends you're only having one more drink.

Sailing on Eggshells

You know what they say: the better you crush up
your eggshells, the less likely it is that a witch will try
to use them as a ship and sink your boat.

OK, so only British sailors say that. But why?

To break this all down a bit more, sailors in the
British navy believed that it was important, after
eating an egg, to crush the shell into minute pieces.
Otherwise, a witch (or evil spirit) could hop into the
boat-like eggshell, head to sea, and cause ships to
sink.

While this sounds like something from a cold
meds-induced dream, this myth has roots that
stretch all the way back to the first century CE, when
the Roman historian Pliny the Elder wrote, in no
uncertain terms, that the act of crushing eggshells
is necessary to avoid being bewitched—though he
stops short of mentioning witches heading out to
sea. Nevertheless, this connection between witches,
eggs, and the sea has existed for centuries, thanks
in part to Pliny's early warnings. One Irish folktale
I found speaks of a particular witch who killed men
at sea from the comfort
of her own home by
putting three eggs
in a pan and, as
they each heated
up and "popped"
out of the pan,

the witch claimed a life. The story goes that three men had drowned nearby that very same day.

Perhaps because of the long-standing associations as well as the trauma caused by widespread witch trials across Europe, the belief in this particular myth has held strong and made eggshell crushing compulsory even among land goers. By the early twentieth century, just about everyone in the United Kingdom was crushing eggshells to do their part to prevent any wicked incidents from occurring out at sea.

No word on why these sorcerers couldn't just reassemble the eggshells and set sail. Let's just be thankful they haven't figured it out yet.

Milk before Sugar

Before you make your next cuppa, keep in mind that whatever moves you can have a major impact on your love life.

In parts of the United Kingdom, adding milk to your tea before adding sugar is a no-go. If you dare be so uncouth, you'll have terrible luck in romantic relationships and never, ever get married.

In the long list of tea-related superstitions, this one strikes me as particularly draconian. To think that one slip-up in terms of preparation, even though it will have no effect on the tea, could have catastrophic effects on your love life seems over the top.

But honestly, it's also kind of terrifying, perhaps made more so because of the frustrating lack of information about where it comes from! I have so many questions! What if you only drink tea with milk and not sugar? What if you use an alternative milk, like oat or soy? What if a drop of milk accidently makes its way into your tea before the sugar does? Is there any hope of redemption, or are you doomed to singledom for life? Also, what if you drink your tea with no milk or sugar at all? Does that mean your love life will be rich and uncomplicated? That's a good thing, right?

There's also the fact that some Brits have historically poured milk into their cups before adding the tea to keep porcelain cups from cracking from the heat. Are there any exceptions when the intent is to maintain your tea set? What disaster does that tradition entail for one's love life?

In the absence of any answers to my burning questions, I'll turn to milk itself. Milk as a substance is typically the first and only thing newborns consume. As such, milk is closely linked to maternalism, bonding, and innocence. This leads me to believe that there's a not-so-feminist message hidden in this superstition: if you pour milk into your tea and then pour sugar in, you're essentially "sullying" the milk;

but if you add the milk last, it's as if it manages to cloak everything else and keep it pure.

A stretch? Perhaps. But maybe the biggest take away from this strange superstition is that life might be a little easier to tolerate if we all stopped reading so much into how people prepare their warm beverages. Drink them as you please and move on with your life!

Candy Makes It Stick

Want to ace a test in South Korea? A sticky candy might be your secret weapon.

It's not uncommon to see students across the country with a piece of *yeot*, a toffee-like confection, as they prepare to take a test. The superstition goes that the stickiness of the candy will help the test taker retain information, which, of course, will lead to a better grade.

While most superstitions are triggered by centuries of external/societal pressure and uncertainty, this sucrose-laden schtick has emerged relatively recently in South Korea thanks to rigorous schooling and the sky-high expectations that have followed. On one hand, the demands from the education system have helped South Korea become one of the most educated countries in the entire world, with roughly 70 percent of its adult population holding at least one higher education degree. On the other hand, the pressure to succeed has also had an

outsized negative impact on young peoples' mental and physical health, including a considerable rise in sleep deprivation and suicides over the last couple of decades.

So, do people in the world's most educated country really believe that chewing on a piece of candy before a test will help retain the correct answers? Probably not. But when the stakes are so high, every little bit helps.

Long Noodles, Long Life

Life is like a noodle. It can be long, tough to swallow, and a little messy. But, for the most part, it's enjoyable.

My simile may be lost on my fellow North Americans, but in China, it's actually the basis of this next superstition. As a staple food across the country, noodles are essentially synonymous with life. So much so that noodles have become a symbol of life itself—the longer the noodle, the longer the life. In fact, people in China sometimes skip the

birthday cake and opt for a bowl of noodles, hoping to manifest a lengthy run.

Because of this link, it's also considered extremely bad luck to cut your noodles at any time, as it means—you guessed it—that your own life will also be cut short. This aversion to cutting noodles even extends to chewing. Instead, it's considered more appropriate and safer to slurp them down.

The origin of this myth seems to date back to the Han Dynasty—which began in 206 BCE and lasted until 220 CE. One potential origin story relates that a group of advisors to the emperor were trying to find a suitable method of determining one's lifespan and suggested measuring the length of one's face. But since this association would cause people to involve themselves in all kinds of dangerous contortions and practices in order to elongate their faces, something a bit more harmless was suggested. Since the word for "face" (liǎn) just so happens to sound like the word for "noodle" (miàn) in Chinese, and because acquiring noodles is far easier than being born with a long face, noodles eventually became the means of evaluating how long one's life would run.

So, instead of being intimidated by a bowl of long noodles sitting in front of you and searching for a fork and knife to make it seem more manageable, perhaps we should all embrace the noodle for exactly what it is, and slurp it up in its messy and delicious gloriousness.

Resources

A handful of the resources, from books to websites, that were particularly useful and insightful through-out the conception of this book:

Diana Wells

100 Birds and How They Got Their Name

Algonquin Books of Chapel Hill, 2002

Harry Oliver

Black Cats & Four-Leaf Clovers: The Origins of Old Wives' Tales and Superstitions in Our Everyday Lives

TarcherPerigee, 2010

Atlas Obscura

www.atlasobscura.com

Culture Trip

theculturetrip.com

Daily Sabah

www.dailysabah.com

Dartmouth Folklore Archive
journeys.dartmouth.edu

History
www.history.com

House of Good Fortune
www.houseofgoodfortune.org

Merriam-Webster Dictionary
www.merriam-webster.com

Reader's Digest
www.rd.com

Smithsonian Magazine
www.smithsonianmag.com

USC Digital Folklore Archives
folklore.usc.edu

About the Author

Shelby El Otmani is a New Hampshire–based writer and radio producer. Shelby's experience in broadcast journalism along with a lifelong interest in psychology inspired her to explore how we develop our beliefs, why they stick with us, and how media and technology impact the decisions we make. Outside of work, you can probably find her surfing, learning kung fu, or hanging out at a coffee shop with a good book.

About Cider Mill Press
Book Publishers

Good ideas ripen with time. From seed to harvest,
Cider Mill Press brings fine reading, information,
and entertainment together between the covers
of its creatively crafted books. Our Cider Mill
bears fruit twice a year, publishing a new
crop of titles each spring and fall.

"Where Good Books Are Ready for Press"

Visit us on online at

cidermillpress.com

Or write to us at

501 Nelson Place
Nashville, TN 37214